The Fire This Time

The Fire This Time

Randall Kenan

 MELVILLEHOUSE

HOBOKEN, NEW JERSEY

Melville House Publishing
300 Observer Highway
Third Floor
Hoboken, NJ 07030

First Melville House Printing: June 2007

www.mhpbooks.com

Book Design: Blair & Hayes

A catalog record for this book is available from the Library of Congress.

for
Jailen
&
Gibreel
&
all the young ones

The Fire This Time

God gave Noah the rainbow sign
No more water, the fire next time!

—Traditional

JAMES ARTHUR BALDWIN was born in Harlem in 1924. The out of wedlock child of a mother from the South, he was adopted by her husband, a store-front Pentecostal minister who raised him along with their children as his own. Baldwin distinguished himself early on as a precocious writer, and also as a child minister. His crisis of faith, which led to his abandoning the pulpit in high school, became the basis for much of his adult writing.

After spending two years living in Greenwich Village and trying to make a living as a reviewer and writer by taking odd jobs along the Northeastern Corridor, Baldwin decided to flee the country of his birth, hoping for a better racial climate and a place where he could concentrate on his writing. In 1948 he settled in post-

World War II France, but found the situation only slightly better in terms of bias against racial minorities, and it was even more difficult to make a living. Through the kindness of friends, especially his lover, the Swiss Lucien Happersberger, Baldwin eventually finished his first novel in a small village in Switzerland. After a time he found an American publisher in Alfred A. Knopf, and in 1953 that novel, *Go Tell It on the Mountain*, was hailed as a critical success and as the debut of an important new voice. Baldwin's next novel, 1956's *Giovanni's Room*, whose main characters were white men and whose theme was homosexual love, was considered highly controversial. Knopf refused to take the book, but, by and by, it found a home first with a British publisher and then with the Dial Press, and was widely admired for its daring.

During this period the self-exiled Baldwin began to visit his home country to cover the accelerating civil rights movement in Arkansas, Alabama, Georgia, and other places. His writings were collected in 1955 as *Notes of a Native Son*, which was considered one of the most articulate accounts not only of the freedom movement but of the state of African Americans in American Society.

The New Yorker commissioned Baldwin to write an article about the Honorable Elijah Muhammad in 1962. The mentor of Malcolm X and the founder of the fast-growing and important Nation of Islam, the religious leader agreed to meet with Baldwin in his Chicago mansion. The resulting account became the basis of the article "Down at the Cross: A Letter from a Region of My Mind" and later the major part of the book *The Fire Next Time*. This 1963 work became an instant best-seller; Baldwin graced the cover of *Time* magazine, and the event marked a significant turning point both in the life of Baldwin and for the civil rights movement.

In the ensuing years Baldwin became a prolific author, publishing four novels—*Another Country* (1962), *Tell Me How Long the Train Has Been Gone* (1968), *If Beale Street Could Talk* (1974), *Just Above My Head* (1979)—four nonfiction works—*Nobody Knows My Name* (1961), *No Name in the Street* (1972), *The Devil Finds Work* (1976), and *The Evidence of Things Not Seen* (1986)—and many plays and short stories. He became recognized as a major voice of Black America and was much in demand as a speaker and lecturer. He became acquainted with such leaders as Martin Luther King, Jr., Malcolm X, Robert F. Kennedy, and with many of the renowned writers, musicians, and actors of his day.

After years of traveling back and forth between America, France, and Turkey, he settled in the south of France, in an estate in Saint Paul-de-Vence, where he lived until his death in 1987.

Baldwin's prose is marked by Biblical rhetoric and a love for nineteenth-century writers, and his elaborate sentences and formal tone gave him a singular style among African American writers. His themes also arose from both *agape* (unselfish love) and a Protestant belief in the power of redemption—a redemption that he hoped would come to his homeland. He held himself to a high standard of truth-telling—hard truths, difficult truths, truths about race—and he admitted that, in a sense, he had never really left the pulpit.

At the end of his seminal essay *Notes of a Native Son*, he wrote:

> It began to seem that one would have to hold in the mind forever two ideas which seemed to be in opposition. The first idea was acceptance, the acceptance, totally without rancor, of life as it is, and men as they are: in the light of this idea, it goes without saying that injustice is a commonplace. But this did not mean that one could be complacent, for the second idea was of equal power: that one must never, in one's own life, accept these injustices as commonplace but must fight them with all one's strength. This fight begins, however, in the heart and it now had been laid to my charge to keep my own heart free of hatred and despair.

A Change is Gonna Come: A Letter to My Godson

One is responsible to life: It is the small beacon in that terrifying darkness from which we come and to which we shall return. One must negotiate this passage as nobly as possible, for the sake of those who are coming after us. But white Americans do not believe in death, and this is why the darkness of my skin so intimidates them. And this is also why the presence of the Negro in this country can bring about its destruction. It is the responsibility of free men to trust and to celebrate what is constant—birth, struggle, and death are constants, and so is love, though we may not always think so— and to apprehend the nature of change, to be able to be willing to change. I speak of change not on the surface but in the depths— change in the sense of renewal.

—*The Fire Next Time*, James Baldwin

Dearest Jailen,

Nine months before you were born, your grandfather, Mr. John Wallace Brown, died.

In every aspect but one, he was my father. I first met him when I was five years old, visiting your grandmother's home in Harlem, USA. He took a shine to me straightaway. Recordings exist of me asking him silly questions ("Can you eat a thousand biscuits?"). He took the entire family to Chinatown, I remember, and he took me to his gym. Your grandfather had been a boxer, but by the time I met him, in his late thirties, he had become a trainer of other boxers. The gym was in uptown Manhattan in the 150s, a dankish, run-down place, smelling of sweat and blood and smelling salts, but it held my fascination for decades. (A few years before he died, I casually mentioned to your mother's father that I had read that the great jazz trumpeter Miles Davis liked to box. Your grandfather said, Of course, he knew that. Davis used the same gym. You saw him, he told me.)

The year your mother was born, your grandfather and grandmother left New York for North Carolina, your maternal homeland. I was ten years old that year.

Many people had an enormous influence on my mischievous mind—undoubtedly the greatest of them being your great-grandmother, who took me in as an infant. But the impact your grandfather had on me was profound.

He had been a civil servant for the City of New York for over twenty years, but he dressed like a duke and carried himself like a crown prince (a large part of that coming from the physical grace he had learned as a boxer; part coming from a certain confidence and leonine heart). He was not himself college educated, but he was more curious about the world than most college professors I would come to know, and he was possessed of a wisdom forged in hand-to-hand combat with life. He bequeathed to me at an early age a love of jazz, especially Wes Montgomery, Billie Holiday, and Sarah Vaughan ("the Divine One"). He respected Dinah Washington the way some people respect the Pope.

He was independent, but not haughty. He believed in decency and courtesy. If someone demonstrated a need, he would lend the proverbial hand, though he was always on the lookout for being taken advantage of. He blamed this ingrained suspicion and a dogged frugality on having been raised during the Great Depression.

He was not a perfect man. He would be the first to admit to a Tasmanian-devil temper. But I never saw him harm anyone, though I well knew he was more than capable.

Chinquapin was and is a small, unincorporated village and the only fire protection is volunteer. Soon after arriving as a full-time resident, your grandfather joined the Fire and Rescue Squad as a fireman. At the time, few of the black men in the community felt welcome on the force, which was founded and run by the local white farmers and schoolteachers and plumbers and truckdrivers who owned homes in the area. But your grandfather often said: If I expect them to come to my house if it's on fire, I should be willing to go to theirs. He studied at the local community college for his certification as a emergency medical technician (I still remember the things he taught me about checking someone's vital signs; about how to deal with someone having an epileptic seizure; about how to staunch the flow of blood and figure out if a fracture is simple or compound.)

Most weekends the Fire and Rescue Squad would hold Saturday benefit suppers selling fried chicken, pork barbecue (a local favorite and specialty), slaw, potato salad, hush puppies. Friday afternoons men would begin slow-roasting the whole hog in a shed behind the firehouse. This process lasted all night. Often on those Friday nights your grandfather would be on call there overnight and would help watch the hog. Many times I would stay with him, and we would roast a chicken along with the hog—wrapped in aluminum foil, drenched in a local sauce, spicy and good, placed among the coals. That chicken still ranks as some of the best food I have ever tasted.

On at least two occasions, in the very wee hours, your grandfather answered calls about accidents involving my classmates. One involving a fatal gunshot wound, one involving a ruinous car wreck. Being there, watching him deal with the death of young people, was an odd place for me; the sorts of events that brace the soul and make you ponder your own mortality and the randomness of life. These were people I knew. On those nights, after delivering the bodies to the hospital, your grandfather would be tired but restless, and he would wax philosophical, speaking of many things, trying in his way to make sense of the world for himself and for me. He was a great talker.

Years later, as an adult, I would come to devote many years to traveling and to writing about African American lives, and to a quest toward understanding the meaning of "blackness," a journey that continues for me. During these wanderings and wonderings I always return to your grandfather and to the many lessons he taught me, both directly and by example. Of the many things I learned from all the people I've written about all across North America, the consonant element about their identity, the thing that forged who they were, what gave them their vision of themselves and the world, was this sense of family, those early people who helped shape who they were—this was the bedrock of their identity. Of course this is true for everyone, of any color, but it is surprising how often we let that truth slip from our thinking. Like them you will need to know a great deal about your past, where you come from, what your people were like—really like—what they thought of you, in order to better understand yourself. You need to know how your own blood lived and faced adversity and of what their character was composed. And though your own journey will no doubt be easier for you than it was for your grandfather and for me, your path will not necessarily be an easy one. So much of that passage will ultimately depend upon you.

For many in the world, in their jaded eyes, alas, now and for many years to come, you will be a demon. For the next thirty years or so you will be among the most despised group in the homeland: the young African American male. *The black male.* This will not be a reality; you are much more than that. But, as an idea, this view of you will have great power. The world will, with a great deal of might and resource, try to define you. But you must know better. You must remember you are not a problem.

These days people can be so trite when discussing the idea of race and its attendant problems. Too many reach instantly for bromides and hackneyed phrases that merely restate positions, rehash old battles, resurrect silly stereotypes. These silly ways of thinking aren't going away anytime soon, but you need not subscribe to them or pay them much heed. The world is no longer—it never really was—about simply black and white. Don't heed people who tell you differently. The old American order of white versus black is fast changing, and you will have a real opportunity (one of the greatest opportunities in history) to break free of such limited thinking. Many people are threatened by this new and burgeoning reality.

But pluralism is the watchword of the future. "Multiculturalism" doesn't come close to encompassing the battles to be waged, the alliances that need to be made. Black folk are no longer the largest minority in this nation, and our continued enduring and prevailing rest with an understanding of how we fit in the new demography. History, alas, does not privilege the people on the side of right; history never does. Might is not always right, but knowledge will always defeat blunt force in the end. Know the past, learn from the past, but don't be a slave to it: Keep moving forward.

In a way—barring some racial cataclysm between now and then—your generation will be the freest people of color this nation has ever engendered: free of racial guilt, free of the burden of representation, free of expectations, high or low—you will not be expected to lift up the race, nor will you be shackled with the hope that your every step will drag along an entire population toward some Promised Land: You will have achieved that land, for better or for worse, borne up on the wings of those who came before. Honor them. Study them. Learn from them. "I may not get there with you..."

You will be like ravens. Free to pick and chose, beautiful, raucous, difficult to control, both trickster and avatar. *Y'all ain't gonna let nobody hold you down. Hold you down. Hold you down.*

Did you know, once upon a time, black folk could fly? Or so it has been said. A hidden truth. A metaphor. A way of looking at yourself and at the world. Remember that when you think you are stuck in the mud.

Your loving godfather,
Randall
Garrett

For now he knew what Shalimar knew: If you surrender to the air, you could ride it.

—*Song of Solomon*, Toni Morrison

Sorrow Songs

In Memphis, Tennessee, on December 3, 1999, Crystal, aged thirty, died. For the next thirty-three days her nine-year-old son, Travis, lived alone with his mother's body. He covered her body with a coat and notebook paper. He fed himself canned soup and breakfast cereals and frozen pizza. When he had no more food he went through the apartment finding whatever money he could and walked himself to buy groceries. He went to school every day—not missing a one—dressing himself, riding the school bus, doing his homework on time. He cut his own hair. He signed his mother's name when he needed to.

When a friend came by with her husband to check on them, for she could not raise anyone on the phone, Travis met them at the door. He is reported as having said: "Mama can't talk anymore because she got really sick and I think she is dead." The prospect of going to a foster home had terrified him. (Later it would be discovered that his mother suffered from a fist-sized, noncancerous tumor in her lung.)

For most of the winter of 2000, this story captured the heart of West Tennessee and much of the nation. People gave money and support. Though it doesn't really matter to point it out, Crystal and Travis were African American. This was one of the saddest, most existential stories I had ever heard. But what does one do with such a tale?

My response was to write a short story about it. Perhaps the impulse sounds a bit cold at first blush, but I wanted to turn this tragic and bizarre narrative into a short story. For me stories are able to make sense when little else can. Not so much in terms of teasing out morals or rigidly defining that which is so elusive and frightening and senseless in the world, but by allowing us to slip into another's soul for a short period, to perhaps comprehend that which is them, to glimpse their experience for a brief while. But for reasons I could not grasp, the fictional daemon eluded me. Perhaps such stories cannot be altered, cannot be mussed with. Perhaps their truth remains somehow inviolate. Realty's starkness sometimes defies recasting. And yet the story continues to move me, to teach me; it is the power of the narrative itself, the emotional force, just like the power of the most straightforward gospel or the rawest blues lament.

Perhaps, when all is said and done, this story will best be expressed as a Sorrow Song.

Through all the sorrow of the Sorrow Songs there
breathes a hope—a faith in the ultimate justice of
things. The minor cadences of despair change often to
triumph and calm confidence. Sometimes it is faith in
life, sometimes a faith in death, sometimes assurance
of boundless justice in some fair world beyond. But
whichever it is, the meaning is always clear: that
sometime, somewhere, men will judge men by their
souls and not by their skins. Is such a hope justified?
Do the Sorrow Songs sing true?

—*The Souls of Black Folk*, W. E. B. Du Bois

In 1903 W. E. B. Du Bois wrote, in his landmark book *The Souls of Black Folk*, "The problem of the Twentieth Century will be the problem of color line—the relation of the darker to the lighter races of men."

A son of Massachusetts, he was educated at Fisk University and was one of the first African Americans to receive a PhD from Harvard University. He became an astoundingly prolific sociologist, novelist, and polemicist; a founder of what would become the National Association for the Advancement of Colored People, and the editor of its important magazine, *The Crisis*, during a time when it was read by a large number of African Americans all across the nation. Du Bois was long-lived, and the older the scholar got it seemed the more radical his views became.

For one of our greatest native-born geniuses he was as right on the point of the color line as he ever was about anything. Some could say he was hedging his bets, figuring that his all-consuming topic could not be so easily solved. Yet, when you consider the changes he had seen—born in 1868, just after the Civil War, witness to slaves becoming members of the United States House and Senate, freedmen beginning with nothing and transforming themselves into substantial landowners, slave boys becoming great scientists, dark women once shackled but now leading the crusade for suffrage; when you consider how much of the twentieth century was still to come in 1903—it is not difficult to see how much of a prophet Du Bois truly was.

That was over one hundred years ago, and after a maelstrom of American societal change, and, despite cries to the contrary, the problem of the twenty-first century will not be a matter of color so much as it will be a matter of class—about access to education, access to funds, access to power; a definition of class that is now more fluid than ever for some, while becoming ever more stratified for others. The new century's biggest problem will not be about assimilation but an all-out assault on the very notion of what it means to be an American. Despite evidence to the contrary, "color" is becoming less and less important, antiquated, though not eradicable, not irrelevant. Bastions of traditional thinking, traditional prejudices, still exist, but these pockets are quickly waning in power, about to go the way of vinyl and eight-track tapes.

What had once been so easily defined as the ongoing black-against-white conflict has metastasized into a polychromatic, polyglot, polyethnic stew of a war. And within the black community, what once had been romantically seen as a monolithic voice from a mountaintop, a series of moral Elijahs and Moseses and Apostle Pauls condemning their pharaohs and Pilates, has broken free of those old Biblical archetypes into a fractal world of politics and economies, a chaos of culture, a bouillabaisse of media, a shifting tangle of strategies and agendas and ideologies. What once had been so easily polarized by Huey Newton and Marcus Garvey is now not so easily parsed.

• • • • •

W. E. B. Du Bois died on August 27, 1963, not only the same year, but the day before the historic March on Washington for Jobs and Freedom, where Bayard Rustin and A. Philip Randolph saw decades of work coming to fruition; where the great photographer Gordon Parks would create iconic images; where famous actors and singers, black and white, would come together as one, from Dylan and Baez to Harry Belafonte and Marian Anderson, and, most famously, where Dr. Martin Luther King, Jr., gave one of the most well-known speeches in history, in fact an extemporaneous speech given after a speech that became better known than the words he had originally penned. While in Accra, Ghana, as a long-term guest of Kwame Nkrumah, the first black head of state of a postcolonial independent African nation, the ninety-five-year-old firebrand gave up the ghost.

Roy Wilkins, who in 1963 was executive secretary of the NAACP, but who had taken over *The Crisis* magazine from Du Bois in 1934, made the announcement to the hundreds of thousands. He said:

> Regardless of the fact that in his later years, Dr. Du Bois chose another path, it is incontrovertible that at the

> dawn of the twentieth century his was the voice that
> was calling to you to gather here today in this cause.

Nearing his death, Dr. Du Bois remained more than a bit disillusioned by the direction race relations were taking in America (as well as by the continuing lack of rights among poor folk, and by the increasingly imperialist streak he saw in the American government). In fact, his exile in Ghana was due to his treatment by the United States government for his more controversial and progressive beliefs and activities, a fact that embittered him. One cannot help but wonder what Dr. Du Bois would have made of the last great racial calamities of the post-civil rights era: the hoopla, the debates, the outsized attention they received, the unexpected passion they summoned.

As J. Edgar Hoover liked to say, Look at your newspapers this morning.

Consider: the O. J. Simpson trial, a latter-day Othello and Desdemona tale, which literally received more mass media attention than most modern wars. Along with when they heard that John F. Kennedy had been shot and when the World Trade Center towers went down, most Americans will be able to tell you where they were when The Verdict was read. Few events in the popular media revealed so clearly the way many white folk felt about black folk, and the way many black folk felt about white folk: simmering mistrust, combative, separate, unequal. Looming larger than the spectacle of a low-speed car chase or high-speed Cult of Personality coverage were the specter of miscegenation, evidence of an unbalanced and biased judicial system, and the legendary fear of police forces among the black community. But more than anything else, the so-called Trial of the Century taught the American public that race relations had not progressed nearly as far as the average citizen had assumed they had. More than a decade later, whenever Simpson raises his head like a wounded grizzly, the media snarls and howls as if he poses a new danger, which makes one wonder how much of the original animus had to do with the belief in an injustice, and how much was a pure and simple case of negrophobia.

Consider the 1992 Los Angeles riots (or Rebellion, depending on your interpretation, and not necessarily confined to California) following the verdict in the case of Rodney King versus the City of Los Angeles Police Department. A key element of that trial had been a videotape of a black man surrounded by police officers with batons, the heart-stopping image of a beating beamed around the world again and again and again. One need not be a Cassandra to have predicted the explosion of rage that made a nation stand still for those chilling hours that ensued; one must be completely out of touch with the American culture to misunderstand that rage.

The story of sundry police departments versus The Black Man captured many a headline during the last decade of the twentieth century: In February of 1999, a West African immigrant named Amadou Diallo was gunned down by four white New York policemen who fired forty-one bullets. On August 9, 1997, a handcuffed Haitian immigrant named Abner Louima, was beaten and sodomized with a broomstick by four white police officers in the bathroom of a Brooklyn police station. Because these two incidents occurred in New York City, the attention they received was exceptional, but similar reports were arising, with less fanfare, from Miami and

Houston and Chicago and Baltimore and Washington, D.C., and
Charlotte and smaller cities. To be sure, although violent crime has
been on the decline, honest-to-God black criminals were not rare—
including some celebrated cases, such as the bizarre case of one Colin
Ferguson, who, on December 7, 1993, in a schizophrenic mania
murdered six people and injured nineteen others on a Long Island
Railroad train. Drug-related crime, domestic violence, grand theft
auto, and a grocery basket of other misadventures committed by
black men, red-handed and guilty, went into the cauldron that
stoked the fears and misgivings of Americans, black and white.

Or consider, in a less violent though no less passionate realm,
the fight over the United States Senate confirmation of Judge
Clarence Thomas as an associate Supreme Court justice in the fall
of 1991. A graduate of Yale University, former chairman of the
Equal Employment Opportunity Commission, a justice on the
U.S. Court of Appeals for the District of Columbia Circuit, this
black man from Pin Point, Georgia, was at once the very embodi-
ment of all the good things an American could achieve; the walking, talking symbol of the American Dream; and, on the other
hand, the golem on which the other half of America visited its
fiercest ire and bile and loathing. Here was a black man who
turned his back on his liberal upbringing, who became a water-car-
rier for the Man, who harassed women employees, and who probably played poker with Beëlzebub. He himself called the media cir-
cus and frankly pornographic testimony at his hearing/inquest a
"high-tech lynching for uppity Blacks." This event revealed the sea
change in the state of Black America, the great divide between the
privileged and the poor, and the shifting, almost unpredictable

allegiances being formed between the Right and the Left. Who speaks for black folk now?

And consider, most recently, the aftermath of the Gulf Coast's fateful encounter with a storm named Katrina, which was followed by another storm named Rita: the American government and its leaders' (black and white) telltale response, the plight of the victims, the rhetoric that has swirled around that tragedy and the ensuing debacle like buzzards circling over a ripe carcass, and all that ongoing jazz. The American media stood aghast and bewildered at the sight of throngs of folk, overwhelmingly African American, stranded in the SuperDome and outside the Ernest N. Morial Convention Center, on highway overpasses and rooftops, waiting one day, two days, three days, and longer; being shot at when trying to find safety in nearby Gretna; seemingly abandoned by the last remaining superpower, of which they were citizens. Of even greater import than the puzzling indifference shown by the commander-in-chief and his minions was the vivid color of the catastrophe. Ultimately, more white folk than black folk were displaced by the storms, but the magnitude of the devastation's consequences for black folk— their utter lack of resources, the degree of their need—was undeniably out of proportion. Watching the coverage and reading and listening to the other media and registering their collective shock, one wondered what country the American Fourth Estate had been covering all these years. Had the circumstances of the black underclass and the victims in New Orleans and its environs been so well hidden? Or was the indifference they were suffering in 2005 merely a continuation of an ongoing indifference?

Was it truly surprising that the majority of New Orleans' urban denizens were poor and black—in a state that is 32 percent black (the national average is 12 percent), and a city that is 67 percent black? Was it surprising that certain media began reporting uncorroborated rumors of black males murdering, raping, and committing all other manner of satanic behavior in the midst of rising water and wartime demands, when their own mothers and daughters and girlfriends were as vulnerable as any? (Ironically, these rumors began as speculations by a black city official, who had no idea that his off-the-cuff thinking-out-loud would find its way onto the airwaves as gospel truth and turn into the vilification of victims, a perception that lingers in the minds of many Americans to this day.) But as devastating, as heartbreaking, as shocking as it was for citizens to bear witness to a botched response to the Gulf Coast storms of 2005, we should be more shocked, devastated, and heartbroken about the slow progress of the rebuilding, all while our great government prosecutes a trillion-dollar war.

And these are just the large cases, the most obvious ones. No less devastating to their victims are the ongoing cases of black high school males in Mississippi, Georgia, and Tennessee, among others places, convicted and imprisoned for statutory rape for having relations with white girls whose age was close to their own; the case of James Byrd, Jr., in Jasper, Texas, who was senselessly and violently murdered—chained and dragged behind a pickup truck for three miles...

The talk surrounding these incidents—and the amount and type of attention they have received—are symptomatic of the current state of race relations in the fifty United States and among its people. So often the rap about race could, with minimal editing, be lifted from the newspapers of any major newspaper of the nineteenth century: fear of the violent black male, dread of miscegenation, poor black folk as victims of their own doings, law enforcement acting like a lynch mob, and underneath it all an abiding loathing and mutual mistrust; a quandary of whom to blame and what to blame, but a decided need to blame some damn body.

• • • • •

Perhaps one day I will write the story of Travis and his mother, of the existential grimness that is so much at the heart of what we all must face: death—the death of our loved ones and our own—without the tools, the wisdom, the aid to grasp it entire; the fear of being taken away to an even worse Hell. In my stumbling attempts, the only tools that I found, in all the vast arsenal of Western culture, of any use to even approach this sad, sad story is that of the blues.

Why the blues? What can the blues do? More than feel-good tunes or ditties to merely uplift the spirits, the blues (a more contemporary term for what Du Bois had termed Sorrow Songs) have been recognized the world over to be an art form on an entirely different level. Blues and gospel, like twins, are ways of looking at the world, of understanding it, apprehending it, and ultimately changing it. The blues are a lesson and an attitude; a road map and a treasure chest. As a testament to its power, African American music remains the single most influential cultural music on the globe.

More than Irish music, Japanese music, Latin, Russian, English, Jewish... everyone, everywhere, knows black American song. This is not an exaggeration.

Grand theories abound as to why this embrace is the case, both in terms of tonal appeal and philosophy—I always point to the fact that the blues are the most aesthetically pleasing form of existentialism afoot, and even more specifically of Christian existentialism. (Even the great French philosophers, Jean-Paul Sartre being the foremost, declared the blues one of the Earth's most profound forms of existentialist expression.)

Or, to be less exalting and more direct about the matter, in the words of the late, great bluesman John Lee Hooker: The blues heal.

When you think on world history, the culmination makes sense. Who better than the enslaved and exploited to create the only art form that at once acknowledges the depth of sorrow, the seeming fickleness of the universe, and the strange human ability to keep on going—the blues, the gospels, the "old Negro spirituals"? ("And the day keeps reminding me, there's a hellhound on my trail.") They give voice to this existential view of life. For black folks, Christianity had always been, effectively, an existential affair—just me and my God. ("Take my hand, precious Lord.") No matter how strong the family bonds or the community ties, always within the tradition was the acknowledgment of aloneness. ("Sometimes I feel like a motherless child.") That may sound hifalutin when juxtaposed with the lives of the people who wrought those sounds out of the depths of their toils and tears, but in truth, that is the way the old folks themselves saw their earthly sojourns. I remember listening to stories at the feet of old women, themselves the daughters of slaves. Other people have heard these homespun blues, seen them made manifest in people's lives. That is why the Sorrow Songs travel so well, from spirituals to gospel to blues to rhythm-and-blues to hip-hop. So much is writ in the name of science and sociology and official history when it comes to the Thousand Nights and a Night Epic of Africans in America; we have been given data, statistics, theories, case studies... but the feeling remains and enthralls, the sense of self, the irreducible fact that this is me. Ultimately the individual is alone. Will he prevail?

Perhaps if I were a songwriter I could begin to do honor to that singular story of Travis and his personal horror, to capture and communicate the pain, to make sorrow into a Sorrow Song with the ability to heal.

But I'm neither a songwriter nor a poet, so I'll just have to trek on in flatfooted prose, and try to make it sing.

Brother Rabbit Versus Brother Fox

"Am I My Brother's Keeper?"

"That rascal!"

My mother (who was my great-aunt, but whom I have always called Mama) said I grew afraid of the darkness due to my cousins' teasing me about the ghost of her husband, my late great-uncle. He was the first person I ever saw die.

When I ask people about their earliest memory, it truly puzzles me when they say it's from preschool, or kindergarten or first grade. Perhaps they are being cautious, but I remember images vividly from ages two and three and, I believe, from earlier. But I have no doubt about three, for that is how old I was when my great-uncle Redden died on my quilt.

When I was six weeks old, I was brought down from Brooklyn, New York, to Duplin County, North Carolina. My parents were unmarried young people, and in 1963, my paternal grandfather, who ran a dry-cleaning establishment, sent for me. Duplin had been the birthplace of both my father and mother, so I was coming home in a way. My grandfather and grandmother lived and thrived in a small town called Wallace, then bustling like a little beehive, sprung up around a railroad depot, a warren of small tobacco warehouses and poultry plants, several stone's throws from Wilmington, mildly famous among certain history enthusiasts for a Revolutionary War scuffle, the Battle of Rockfish Creek, and home to some magnificent classical American churches and some impressive graveyards.

Very early on, my great-aunt, Mary Fleming, found favor with me. Her only daughter was grown and away in New York, so she and her husband would take me on the weekends to their Chinquapin farm, about fifteen miles east of Wallace, the place where she and my grandfather had grown up. Deep, deep country, on the edge of the Angola swamp, it lay on a dirt road, surrounded by fields and woods. My first memories of the place are apple trees, grapevines, pine trees, and an oak tree so large it could blot out the sun, with limbs as thick as small automobiles, a trunk of truly elephantine proportions. My infant stays there grew longer and longer until, one day, Old Field Road became my home.

Redden Hall was a tobacco farmer. He raised hogs and chickens as well, but tobacco was his main cash crop. Mama had inherited land, and along with her own acreage and some that he leased from others, he ran quite a large operation.

He was a tall, sturdy, redbone man with a jolly and inviting face, easy to smile, and with a purposeful gait. A gentleman in his early fifties. Among my memories while he lived: driving, soon in the morning, in the pitch black, to Wilson, North Carolina, to sell cured tobacco; my first taste of Vienna sausages in his truck parked in the middle of a field, pink they were and salty; my first spanking—how it affronted me!—for having the temerity to move a shovel I was told not to touch; eating sautéed onions with just salt and pepper, a flavor that still haunts me and causes me to think philosophical thoughts; his lessor's son surprising me, while I played on the grass, when the horse he was riding gently nuzzled me from behind: three-year-olds should never be startled face-to-face by a large beast. How could I forget such things?

One day Mama and Redden and I were out by the barn (it was actually referred to as the crib). Redden had an adult son from a previous marriage: Billy, the very image of his father, light skinned, light eyes, booming voice. That day, while the men and Mama conversed, I played under the grape arbor, lost in whatever three-year-olds tend to lose themselves doing with sticks and stones and worms. To my surprise I heard Redden's tractor start up and drive away. I thought Redden had taken off and left me behind. When I ran to see, there I saw Billy, now riding away in the distance, down the dirt road, waving at us. I stood aghast, having clearly digested the notion of ownership and theft (though not their nuances), and I pointed toward the "stolen" tractor and hollered, "The rascal!"

This story was often repeated during my childhood. Perhaps that is why and how I remember it so well.

In those bygone days, after tobacco was harvested it was cured in large barns, hung from rafters, and slowly cooked for about a week by the heat of propane burners aligned on the ground. When they became brown and supple and valuable, the leaves were carefully removed and stacked in great mounds and tied in bales of burlap and then taken to what was called a pack house. Near the end of the season, as summer began to wane, women would be dispatched to the pack house to separate the leaves according to quality. This process was called grading.

I remember, that particular late September day, Mama brought an old quilt—made by her mother—for me to play on while she and the ladies went about their task. This pack house was an old residence, whose I do not know, a small, gutted house of only a few rooms, packed full of dry tobacco. I wandered about watching in the dusty rooms, asking primary questions, inhaling the sweet tobacco musk.

Not very long into the morning my uncle said he wasn't feeling at all well. He was feeling funny. My mother spread out the quilt she had brought on the front porch for him to lie down on. I remember thinking: You brought that for me. I remember saying: "That's my quilt." But generosity, or some sense of sharing, overcame me, and I decided to keep my uncle company and lay down next to him. I think Mama told me to watch over him while they worked. He went to sleep beside me. By and by one of the ladies came to check on him. He wouldn't wake up.

I don't remember exactly when I stopped being afraid of the dark. It was a gradual process. But there were many years—and I never full understood why—where the dark unknown held terrifying possibilities. Was it death I feared, or simply sleep?

· · · · ·

What was once known as the Black Old Guard has never been so irrelevant as it is today. What, you might ask, is the Black Old Guard?

To this date, the most lavish popular-culture representation of that vaunted group—of any consequence—that I can remember was captured in the book and the motion picture *Midnight in the Garden of Good and Evil*. No matter what you thought of the book or the movie, there appeared—mid-book, mid-movie—this curious phenomenon: a black debutante ball. A cotillion. A coming-out soiree— coming out to society as an eligible, marriageable young woman. White folk of a certain ilk (and age) will appreciate at once what these signifiers mean. But for the vast majority of twenty-first century Americans such a phrase, such an unlikely combination of meanings, means little. Light-skinned Southern black aristocrats, high-born daughters and sons of doctors, lawyers, bankers, postmasters, and in some cases schoolteachers, but more, members of a Certain Crowd, shrouded in codes and genealogical lore. To belong to such a club, to this rarified caste, one has to be born into it, with precious few exceptions. These rituals were created to make certain that the Circle will be unbroken. This was/is a world of social status that seems oddly out of step, a world where lineage counts for more than it does among the peers of Europe, a world where even racial language is encoded, and where one might be unaccountably proud to have had a great-great-great-grandmother who was essentially used by a landowner who had himself inherited his way in the world. Though this peculiar society largely still finds its legs in the larger cities of the American South— Savannah, Atlanta, Charleston, New Orleans, Jacksonville, Birmingham, Nashville, Richmond, Durham—the world of the Black Old Guard was never limited to the South, finding important branches among the Black Brahmins of Boston, the Strivers of Harlem's Striver's Row and Edgecomb Avenue, even in Los Angeles' Baldwin Hills. The Old Guard has endured as a national sub-subculture, however marginalized, however marginal it has always been. So tiny that it is almost invisible. So inbred and subliminally self-loathing that it has almost become comic to those who are aware of it—comic if it weren't so curiously tragic. In this e-mail-ridden, Tivo-laden, IPod-listening world, the very notion of a black middle class defined by a combination of skin color and a blood connection to a rich white person seems not only quaint, but a bit ridiculous. But sadly, this was—and for some still is—serious bidness.

• • • • •

I first learned of this subculture when I was in high school. I was just coming out to myself as a bibliomane and, a kid lost in the swamps of eastern North Carolina, I had become a friend of book clubs, those buy-four-books-for-a-dollar-and-join-our-club clubs. There, in the monthly booklet that arrived announcing the DOUBLEDAY BOOK CLUB SELECTION OF THE MONTH and the library of books available for my hard-earned tobacco- and grass-cutting money, was a book by Stephen Birmingham: *Certain People: America's Black Elite*. The jacket copy read in part:

> This book is about the heritage, conflicts, and charac-
> teristics of the black upper class in America. The way
> they dress, decorate their homes, eat, and raise their
> children. Birmingham, a scholar of black history,
> genealogy and sociology, offers a comprehensive view
> of the emergence of a stratified black society. The
> black, white relationships in business, recreation, and
> social functions...

(Lawrence Otis Graham updated that self-same world in a more detailed and personal manner in his 1999 book, *Our Kind of People: Inside America's Black Upper Class.* Himself a member, himself a scion of a Southern aristocratic black family, himself the product of Princeton and Harvard Law, Graham had an insider's view of real estate and social clubs, the talented tenth of a tenth who rule certain Historically Black Colleges, more social clubs, and more real estate—primarily vacation spots. His account is not radically different from the one proffered twenty years before, aside from reporting a better fashion scene.

(It is worth noting, also, that Graham had burst on the scene a few years earlier with an article published in *New York* magazine in which he reported on his "going under cover" as a waiter at a posh, unofficially whites-only country club in Westchester County. Here he was, an Ivy League-educated, Wall Street lawyer, playing a servant for white folk who treated him like—a servant! For some reason this astounded Mr. Graham. He went on to write a book, *Member of the Club*, about this degrading experience.)

But in the raw, wonderful days of 1977, when I was heading to North Carolina Governor's School, science-bound, ambition-stuffed, my head awash with notions of becoming a scientist/engineer/captain-of-industry, perhaps a black Howard Hughes, this discovery was a blueprint for something. What, exactly, I could not say. At that point my world was one of hard work and hardscrabble people: farmers, mill workers, a handful of still-sharecroppers. To be sure, scattered among them were a quantity of teachers and a pinch of doctors, and administrators. But nothing like the fancy world in far-off Chicago and Boston and New York City that I was reading about. Suffice it to say that to read about black folk who were not poor, who were movers and shakers and who seemed to have some Voice in the Big World (they were friends of governors and presidents, and they were ambassadors and members of the board) was, in the initial rush, intoxicating. This meant powerfully to me.

For a dirt-poor, illegitimate black country boy, growing up amid the snake- and deer-infested swamps of Duplin County, North Carolina, when *Certain People* arrived I devoured it, so strange and unusual, and somehow instructive, it was; this vision of a high-born, high-living colored aristocracy fascinated my eyes. For years afterward I sought to emulate, replicate, to achieve this rarefied world, in some measure, despite my low origins and lack of M.O.N.E.Y. I really didn't know any better. Besides, it had worked for John H. Johnson.

•••••

In 1977, every black kid who knew how to read knew who John H. Johnson was. For a brief but shining time he became an obsession for me. The richest black man in America. Founder and president and publisher of the Johnson Publishing Company. *Ebony*. *Jet*. Fashion Fair Cosmetics. The Supreme Life Insurance Company. The first black person on the *Forbes* 400 in 1982. $500,000,000. Born poor and dark (as dark as I) in rural Arkansas. Pawning his mother's furniture for $500 to launch his first magazine, *Negro Digest*, in 1942. Shrewd. Lucky. Hardworking—obsessively so. Johnson becomes an even more romantic figure to me over the years, though increasingly problematic. Without a doubt his legend is emblematic of all those capitalist, Protestant ideals Americans like to hold up to the world as proof positive of their worth, of their right to world dominance: Theirs is a country in which the grandson of a slave can become rich and powerful, friend of presidents and consul to foreign lands. Moreover, Johnson created something of great and enduring substance. *Ebony* and *Jet* still reach millions of African Americans. Just as in my childhood, at this writing it would be a challenge to find a barbershop or a beauty parlor in a black neighborhood that is not littered with back issues of both. At the apogee of the civil rights movement in the sixties Johnson's publications were at the zenith of their penetration among the black nation-within-a-nation as well as at the forefront of journalism at large, with the publication of the Emmett Till photographs perhaps being the most bracing—and galvanizing—in the history of the black press.

JPC and its many publications were also a platform—much in the same way Henry Luce used *Life* and *Time*—for Johnson's vision of the triumphant black bourgeoisie, a vision heavy on huge houses, big salaries, expensive weddings, and firsts: first black this and first black that. It was a form of journalism that had a certain power and uplift during Jim Crow, and even in its immediate aftermath, but which now feels a little embarrassing and beside the point; someone has to be first. But are they worthy? Are they the best?

As I grew older, I began to see inherent contradictions in Johnson's emphasis on materialism, his tacit support of the Old Guard's obsession with bloodlines and traditional "belonging"; his willingness to play footsie with any and all administrations as long as they were in power, while simultaneously deifying the great Lion(s) of the Struggle; or, as Earl Long once said of one of his political opponents, talking out of both sides of his mouth at the same time. These elements do not mix well.

One of Johnson's contemporaries had put his finger on the growing unease I was feeling. E. Franklin Frazier (a student of W. E. B. Du Bois) had been the head of sociology at Howard University since the 1930s. He was at times a vehement critic of the mores and preoccupations of the black middle class, and his 1957 *Black Bourgeoisie: The Making of the Black Middle Class* created a firestorm that still rages in some quarters. His was a take-no-prisoners attitude, and he condemned what he saw as pure folly, caprice, rank materialism, and a lack of political and financial substance. Though he identifies what he sees as an overriding problem of economics and self-identify in the treatment of the former slaves and property-ownership during the Reconstruction, and what he sees as self-delusional aspects of the free blacks during slavery, Fraizer comes down hard on a lack of seriousness among black businesses (not manufacturing anything of great worth; focusing on petty retail; scavenging the black community via funeral homes and insurance companies), a boosterism that outstripped reality, and obsessions with things like skin color, social standing, status symbols, and "make-believe." Though the tone of the final chapters of his book are particularly harsh—this in a time when black folks were expected to be criticizing white folk, not black—he meant his scold as a wake-up call, not as a knife to the heart. Needless to say, many of those at whom his most stinging statements were aimed did not find a lot to admire in the professor's castigations.

One of the overarching criticisms of Fraizer's own criticism is that he saw the black bourgeoisie entire, single-minded, and failed to differentiate between those lost in the status game and skin color, and those who were serious-minded, hardworking, and committed to tangible uplift of black folk (and, more problematic, between them and the probably large group that overlapped significantly). One thinks of the Kings of Sweet Auburn Street, Atlanta, who were well-propertied enough to send their scion, Martin, Jr., to Boston University after he graduated from Morehouse. Or the Bonds, or the Jacksons of that city. Or the even more well-heeled Powells of Harlem, whose Adam, Jr., would not only become the most electrifying minister from the pulpit of Abyssinian Baptist Church but one of the most powerful politicians in the United States House of Representatives of the last century, black or white. The black middle class was never monolithic, nor totally lacking in substance.

When I first came across Alex Haley's *Roots*, no less affecting than (though perhaps not as overwhelming as) stories of kidnap, torture, forced labor, rape, and family dissolution was the story of Haley's grandfather, who built and ran a successful lumber mill, and of Haley's father, who became a college professor. The town of Henning, Tennessee, not too far from Memphis, became a thriving small town largely of black folk. That success in the generations that followed Kunta Kinte and Miss Kizzy is what ultimately made *Roots* and Haley's story resonate so with its vast readership as an epic of hope rather than as the tragedy it could so easily have remained. The validity of many of Fraizer's arguments notwithstanding, the complexity and still-promise of the black middle class (in Fraizer's day a skinny 30 percent, but now over 50 percent of the overall black population) cannot be so easily minimized, marginalized, and mistaken.

These visions of, for, and about black-middle-classdom continue with us, grow even more complex, and now have achieved even more mythologically American overtones. Who knows but that on the lower frequencies, Jay Gatsby was black?

Can a Rabbit Skin a Fox?

When Mama's daughter Edythe and her husband Mr. Brown moved with their infant daughter to Chinquapin in 1973, they built a house. A brick house with beige trim, it had four columns in the front which made it, to me, mighty impressive, like an old-timey Big House of Brick. That and the two-car garage.

They purchased acreage about two miles from the family farmhouse, where they lived while their house was being erected. Great pines—many of them long leaf—massive, soaring, ancient towers— were felled. The land was then bulldozed, cleared, made as smooth as a sheet of paper. The house went up mid-lot. At the back, in an area that covered half an acre, easily, was a primordial pyramid, a conglomeration of tree stumps and immature trees and woodland refuse, high and tangled, dark and forbidding—but at the same time lush and wild. I had never seen such a vast and chaotic mound. It reminded me of something from a Grimm's fairy story, especially at dusk. Surely witches and goblins lived therein.

Mr. Brown and Edythe received much advice on how to deal with that mass. Folk said the Neanderthal stumps would have to be blasted away with dynamite. They said bulldozers and trucks would most certainly need to be hired to remove most of the tonnage. This is how others had handled similar situations. It was the done thing. Names were floated of people who were experts in just this manner of heavy work. Quotes were quoted. The good men and women of Chinquapin looked upon Mr. Brown, this city boy, this foreigner in their Old World, this man who had initially mistaken tobacco plants for gigantic collard greens, and who had grown up in Harlem, and they assumed not only that he was overwhelmed by such a Herculean task, but that he would be clueless about how to remedy it.

He listened to their sage council patiently, absorbing all the advice, the facts and figures, the testimony of how such a thing should be handled—all sound wisdom and given with compassion—and, like Big Daddy in *Cat on a Hot Tin Roof*, Mr. Brown simply said: Bull.

Quietly he went about the job, just as the New Year rang in, like a resolution, like a covenant, and with the most rudimentary of tools: axe, pickaxe, shovel, wheelbarrow, maybe a saw (his tool box grew over the months). Thinking back, now older than he was at the time, I'm daunted by the notion, and I was pretty daunted by the project as a boy.

Of course people knew next to nothing about this gentleman, other than that he was a gentleman, didn't drink or smoke, was a snappy dresser, spoke with a New York accent, found their folkways amusing and often downright bizarre; he ran down the dirt roads most mornings, quite early, in sweatclothes—the height of curious behavior in those days. ("I looked to see, and won't nobody or nothing chasing him either!")

To my preteen eyes the idea of the Pile, as we came to call it, was a permanence. Something so large, so jumbled and without a treasure map, something you could not walk over or see over, would clearly take years if not eons to remove. About this I had little doubt.

Every day after school I would join him. As his house slowly took shape, he would be out back, every day, chopping, sawing, digging, burning, burning, burning. Initially, the dents he made looked minuscule. He would show me every log moved, every stump dug out, every bush vanquished. Before long the Pile existed in my mind like the blueprint of some dragon's lair, smoke always belching toward the sky.

During this period I really got to know Mr. Brown, to see many of his moods, hear tales of his growing up in Harlem, of his multi-ethnic schoolmates (black folk, Italian folk, Jewish folk, Irish folk); of his philosophies about work and money and God and love. No grownup had ever spoken to me like this, taken such time and interest in a way that made me feel, if not equal, then able to understand, to process, to remember, to think.

The thing that would amaze me about Mr. Brown and the Pile was the gradualness of it, the day-by-day, one-whack, one-branch, one-shovel-at-a-time nature of the work. A constant series of smoldering fires. Every day. Only raindrops and Sundays would take him from the job. No heed to the naysayers in the community. No discouragement over physical injury. In fact, the more he worked, the more his enthusiasm seemed to grow. It became infectious, and I longed to be out there with him—as difficult and forbidding as the work sometimes felt.

And then, one fine day...

After the mild North Carolina winter, as spring began to grow, where once loomed an ugly temple of distorted wilderness now stretched a fertile plot of earth, barren now but fecund, black soil rolling back to the forest beyond. There Mr. Brown and Edythe planted corn and cucumbers, strawberries, collards and cabbages, string and butter beans, watermelons and peas. Okra.

Dynamite, he would say, looking upon his work, and laugh.

•••••

"'Skin me, Brer Fox,' sez Brer Rabbit, sezee, 'snatch out
my eyeballs, t'ar out my yeras by de roots, en cut off
my legs,' sezee, 'but do please, Brer Fox, don't fling me
in dat brier-patch,' sezee."
—"How Mr. Rabbit was too Sharp for Mr. Fox,"
Joel Chandler Harris

Joel Chandler Harris. Pablo Picasso is reported to have once said: "Good artists borrow, great artists steal." Does that make Joel Chandler Harris a great artist?

Born sometime in the mid-1840s, Harris, a white man, was a Georgia newspaper writer and editor. Between 1881 and his death in 1908, he gave the world a great many volumes of folk tales and sketches. He gave us Uncle Remus.

Published in 1881, *Uncle Remus: His Songs and Sayings* ranks with D. W. Griffith's *Birth of a Nation*, as being as good as it is wicked. Both perpetuate the worst of the late nineteenth century's racist conceptions of black folk, yet both are indelible contributions of form and technique without which the American landscape would be the poorer. In fairness, Harris' racism may have been tempered by a genuine sense of humanity. But his brain was so ensnared by racist thought that even his most humane representation of black folk—exemplified by the character of Uncle Remus—is rank with condescension, a view of the Negro as inferior, avuncular at best. And Harris' sin was compounded by his "borrowing" of the stories he gathered from the former slaves he interviewed and whose trove of African stories, their legacy, marinated in two centuries of bondage and toil, peppered with Native lore, European plots, and the green landscape of the American South and its fauna. And Harris ransacked them with aplomb.

Uncle Remus is an old black retainer of a plantation destined for ruin by the War of Northern Aggression. Salty. Wise. Sweet as sugarcane. Full of stories. In his humble cabin he spins yarns for the benefit of a little white boy who becomes the recipient—as did generations of real children—of untold centuries of Yoruba, Ibo, Hausa, Bantu, Ashanti, and many other cultures' fables and parables brought over in the bellies of slave sloops, in the hearts and minds of kidnaped men and women (some stories actually dating back to that most renowned of African slave tale-spinners, Aesop) and on these shores mingled with the tales of the indigenous folk those Africans encountered. As with most morality folk tales, these stories were peopled by animals, the archetypes for certain human qualities.

What had been lions and monkeys in West Africa became the 'possums and bears of North America. The most famous avatars being Brer (Brother) Rabbit and Brer Fox; and their most well-known tangle being that of Brer Rabbit's succumbing to a certain mute stranger made of tar; once punched, the Rabbit is stuck fast to the silent tormentor. Whereupon up jumps Brer Fox, full of glee and mirth over his chief—though ill-suited—rival's predicament. ("You bin runnin' roun' here sassin' atter me a mighty long time, but I speck you done come ter de een' er de row.") But, in a moment of reversal worthy of Sophocles and Hitchcock combined, Brer Rabbit convinces Brer Fox to abandon him to the horrors of the briar patch, there to die a pitiful, slow death. But the trick is on the fox: "'Bred en bawn in a brier-patch, Brer Fox—bred en bawn in a brier-patch!'" Brer Rabbit proclaims. "En wid dat he skip out des ez lively as a cricket in de embers."

Ironically, along with the fame and influence his stories would engender over the decades as they became part of the American culture, Harris—along with his contemporary Samuel Clemens—made African American speech a literary thing, made it a part of the great big American canon. From that moment in history, Western culture would never recover. "At least it is a fable thoroughly characteristic of the Negro," Harris writes in the introduction to *Uncle Remus*, "and it needs no scientific investigation to show why [the Negro] selects as his hero the weakest and most harmless of all animals, and brings him out victorious in contests with the bear, the wolf, and the fox. It is not virtue that triumphs, but helplessness; it is not malice, but mischievousness." Or at least that is how Harris saw both the tellers of the tale and the beings being told. Remember: Both rabbit and fox are tricksters. For the West African cultures from which these characters sprang, the trickster spirit was holy, the anima in every human being. In most of their tales all animals were tricksters to some degree, often in inverse proportion to their size and strength and authority. Often the wee spider was represented as the greatest trickster of all—Anansi. And it remains revered in many African cultures. One must never kill a spider, they will tell you in Ghana.

Brer Rabbit (a hare back in Africa), is sleek, charming, quick-witted, undeniably fun-loving, and lucky, lucky, lucky.

Brer Fox is a beautiful predator, powerfully intelligent, grace-fully agile, skilled at cunning and treachery.

In Harris' world, despite interpretations to the contrary, both creatures are stand-ins for black folk. This point is important. This point is ur-African. This point is the point.

• • • • •

Rabbits are not only lucky, but they are the masters of mother wit. One of the abiding truths that arise from the study of Africans in North America is the continuing wave not merely of luck, but of a native genius that has saved Black America again and again in the face of families being literally torn asunder and of lynching and of Jim Crow discrimination; luck alone cannot address this epic story. Not that this strategy never failed—it has been thwarted often. Yet those ringing moments of success have been enough to buoy up an entire population.

It is easy to see why the ex-slaves who spoke to Joel Chandler Harris told him tales of Brother Rabbit with such relish (the preva-lence of the hare in West African lore surely being the main reason). Brother Rabbit would not only have been attractive to them, easily identified with: Despite his caprice and his laissez-faire attitude toward life, he is at once weak and powerful, and so easily seen as free. His vulnerability is apparent, yet his routes to escape, his track record in escape, would have been mighty appealing. And what can appeal to the present-day African American at large more than those qualities: mirth in the face of danger; charm, wit, and the skills to escape and live to laugh?

Historically speaking, black folk have much to gaze back upon and learn from in that rare, wonderful brand of hare gumption: Be it the thousands who literally escaped bondage, be it the many who rose up during the Reconstruction to positions of political and financial power—former slaves, a fact that should not be easily forgotten; be it the coping strategies used during the rise of the Klu Klux Klan and the Redemption Period at the tail end of the nineteenth century, and during the imposition of Jim Crow throughout the conquered lands where most black people lived; be it the bedevilments those de facto slaves of segregation visited upon a smug white South and a placid North; be it the movements, organizations, clubs, gangs, church groups, nightclubs, unions, guilds, and lodges that these people formed and wielded under the glare of proto-apartheid to make their voices heard. And in the face of such obstacles they created some of the best colleges in the country and produced some of the best educators, scientists, doctors, lawyers, soldiers, craftsmen, architects, and inventors this country has ever known. From cattlemen to engineers, from surgeons to gardeners, they not only endured, but prevailed. One could wallow in the appreciation of the success of those sons and daughters of the slaves and of their grandchildren. So easily can it be forgotten how soon after their bondage they rose up, were struck down, and rose up yet again.

Strangely, in the last forty years, despite an array of black folk who have continued within that proud tradition, a broad swath of their descendants are not striving, achieving, transcending in that same fashion. Sadly they seem to be going backward, and at an alarming rate.

One only need look at the sobering statistics to see how bleak that plight is 143 years after emancipation.

According to the National Urban League's most recent State of Black America report, Black America as a whole lags behind White America by a significant amount, and the gap is widening. For anyone who reads the newspapers or who watches CNN, this fact should not be surprising. One might even say it is not news. The real question remains, stubbornly, why?

Why are the unemployment rates for black youth so much higher than the national average? Why do black folk rely on public transportation at four times the rate that white folk do? Why is the high school dropout rate in high school so high among African Americans? Why do black males in the court system receive longer sentences, on average, than do white males? Why is the same true for black females? Why do African Americans pay higher mortgage rates on average? Why are black males "crowded" in lower-paying, unskilled jobs? Why is the number of black children living at or below the poverty level increasing annually? Why are more black men in prison (now approaching one million, the proportion in comparison to white prisoners is far askew: Out of a population of over 2 million inmates, African Americans make up to close to half that number, though African Americans only represent 12 percent of the

U.S. population) than are in college (almost 12 percent of the entire black male populace between the ages of 25 an 29 are locked up)? And what can explain the disturbing rise of HIV infection among young black men? (50 percent of all new cases in 2003 were detected in black men; the Centers for Disease Control estimate that one in three black gay men are HIV positive; the total of estimated cases for African Americans exceeds the cumulative number for that of the entire population of white folk—379,279 in a population approaching 40 million compared to 375,155 in a population of more than 200 million.) Wat can explain the silence about black folk among black folk, especially among once-proud institutions such as the Black Church?

Such lists, whose origins go back to Du Bois' own studies in the 1890s (he is, in fact, widely recognized as a founder of the study of sociology), can be not only startling, but can numb the mind. Yet that would be only part of the story. Positive news abounds: The black middle class—in terms of what the government deems middle class—accounts for half the African American populace, and that number increases; there are more black women in colleges and universities than ever, and their numbers, too, are growing; more black folk are receiving advanced degrees than ever before; more black folk are in managerial positions—with the ability to hire and fire and effect institutional positions—than ever before.

If you walk among black folk—in the churches, in the projects, at the workplace, at the dance joints and bars and corner stores—if you talk to people, one-to-one as I have done quite doggedly over the years—you are not so consumed by dread and despair, as the numbers might lead a thinking person to be. Black folk in all walks of life are aware of the numbers, the statistics; they have a sense of the looming peril facing the vast numbers of their brothers and sisters. Even the billionaires and NBA stars find the statistics hard to avoid. But what you come away with is a sense that this too can be overcome. For better or for worse, one finds the spirit of Brother Rabbit alive and well—a condition at once exasperating and encouraging. *They ain't gonna let nobody hold 'em down. Hold 'em down. Hold 'em down.*

• • • • •

Make no mistake: Brother Fox has been an equal part of Black America from the moment the first slave was taken from the first slave ship. Gabriel Prosser, Denmark Vesey, perhaps even Nat Turner could tell us a lot about Brother Fox. From the pulpit to the plantation kitchen, from the halls of Congress to the drug-selling corners, from the engineering booths to the boardrooms, Brother Fox has been, and continues to be, alive and well.

After Lyndon Johnson (who appointed the first black man to the United States Supreme Court: "The right thing to do, the right time to do it, the right man and the right place"), left office, the cabinet of his successor, Richard Nixon, was practically lily-white, as was that of Gerald Ford. James Earl Carter would enfranchise more black federal officials than any of the thirty-eight chief executives who preceded him. He appointed a black woman as his secretary of housing and urban development and then moved her to secretary of health, education and welfare; he also sent two black men to be ambassador and representative to the United Nations, along with a great many other posts and federal judgeships. When Ronald Reagan came along—only the third U.S. president in the twentieth century (after FDR and Nixon) to receive a clear mandate from the electorate, winning forty-nine states, which made him one of the most formidably powerful politicians in American history—something perplexing happened. Regan did have one black cabinet member (Samuel R. Pierce of HUD), but in the background, one by one, one EOC appointment, one civil rights Commission at a time, not only in the corridors of the executive office building, but on M Street and K Street, and on Wall Street and Centre Street, a new type of black politico was beginning to emerge, funded and dispatched by organizations like the Heritage Foundation and the Hoover Institution of War, Revolution and Peace. This new class of black conservative was not unprecedented, but could safely be called a rare breed until it became, as the fortieth president enjoyed saying, "morning in America." The presence of these men and women inside—and outside—government slowly began to alter the discussion of race in America in ways undreamt of in 1959.

If one's sympathies lie with the Left and a progressive vision of American politics, one might be accused of sour grapes at the least, if not of being vindictive, when one recognizes this trend. However, an assessment of this new species of political operative might lead one to another view of the political landscape and these people's role in it. One must consider, historically speaking, how the right wing of American politics (interestingly enough once firmly entrenched in the Democratic party when it came to segregation and the civil rights of black folk) after taking up residence in the once libertarian-minded Republican party, was essentially Matter to the Antimatter of

Black Power. Even the most "small-c" black conservative would have found little in common with Strom Thurmond or George Wallace. But they were Democrats. The more well-heeled, religiously rectitudinous, and family-oriented might have seen eye to eye with Nelson Rockefeller or even the then-governor of California, Ronald Reagan. But they were Republicans. As were most of the few registered black men and women until the political shifts of the sixties— the Republican party had been the party of Lincoln, and that attachment held a long loyalty for black folk for over one hundred years.

When LBJ rammed through Civil Rights Legislation in 1964, he prophesied that he had given the South to the Republican party for a generation. But it was the right thing to do.

Forty years later, and a lot of games of musical chairs later, those once clearly seen and understood battle lines were no longer so clear. The Republicans had become married to the notion of conservatism; the Democrats had officially adopted black folk—and gay and Native American and Green and physically handicapped, and sometimes what was left of the Labor movement, and anybody else who feared corporate imperialism. And black people, increasingly, were all over the place. One of my college classmates went to work for Jesse Helms, who had once vowed that no one like me—or my classmate—would ever enter the University of North Carolina. Helms failed, and years later he hired this black graduate of UNC-Chapel Hill, Claude Allen, as his 1984 campaign spokesman. Curiouser and curiouser!

At this point in our passage, such happenings do not raise an eyebrow, do not cause much of a fuss except amongst a few who pay too much attention and try to make sense of the scene. And today, black folk are in places of true power. Who knows? Perhaps they are spies in the enemy camp. After all, that is the nature of Brother Fox.

Who knows where the current secretary of state's—the former national security advisor's—allegiances lie, when she fails to speak out on issues affecting most Black Americans domestically? After all, her job is to watch the rest of the world. Who knows what was in Ward Connerly's mind and heart, when the businessman, self-described conservative, and twelve-year regent of the University of California system pushed so heavily for Proposition 209, which effectively ended affirmative action for all state institutions? Who knows what Armstrong Williams, a radio talk-show host, television talking head, and newspaper columnist, was thinking when he accepted hundreds of thousands of dollars from the Bush administration to flack their positions while not sharing the truth of his employment with his thousands of listeners? Who knows what the second-ever black Associate Supreme Court Justice Clarence Thomas, whose hard-won appointment remains as tightly wound round him as his black robe, is really thinking? He doesn't say very much, as people who cover the SCOTUS report. Who knows? What might seem strange bedfellows to some may seem another form of racial progress to others.

Also, in the late 1980s, along with the new conservative black political operative, a new breed of black conservative intellectual came to the fore, with so much energy and verve one might think someone had been holding them back all those years. Intellectual with a capital "I," these men and women were armed with the best education money (or in some cases affirmative action-aided grants and scholarships) could buy, they wrote books, appeared on talk shows, in some cases produced documentaries. On the one hand their basic message did not stray too far from that of the honorable Booker T. Washington and his words known as the Atlanta Compromise. A favorite and recurring theme borrowed from the Wizard of Tuskegee has been "lift yourself up by your bootstraps."

"Cast down your buckets where you are!" Washington chanted:

> The wisest among my race understand that the agitation of questions of social equality is the extremest folly, and that progress in the enjoyment of all the privileges that will come to us must be the result of severe and constant struggle rather than of artificial forcing. No race that has anything to contribute to the markets of the world is long in any degree ostracized. It is important and right that all privileges of the law be ours, but it is vastly more important that we be prepared for the exercise of these privileges. The opportunity to earn a dollar in a factory just now is worth infinitely more than the opportunity to spend a dollar in an opera-house.

Interestingly enough, Dr. Du Bois didn't cotton much to that passage. In fact he despised such an idea. On many things Du Bois and Washington saw eye to eye, contrary to what the famous myth of their feuding relationships suggests, but on the idea of gradualism—

Washington's idea that black folk should climb the ladder of integration into American society slowly—they vehemently disagreed. "Now" was the only acceptable time frame for the good professor. This matter was not, to Du Bois, simply a matter of social engineering: It was a right and a debt owed the former slaves and their sons and daughters. Where Washington was the ultimate American pragmatist, DuBois was the ultimate American moralist.

At root none among the black people who are responsible, hardworking and taxpaying find much to object to in the "up by your bootstraps" notion. But it is worrisome that this new and foxy elite of black conservatives largely denounces and dismisses most of the Great Society programs launched by Lyndon Baines Johnson and his obedient congress; they not only urge the eradication of any and all affirmative-action initiatives, but they help lead the way in eradicating them. Most of their types of intervention are categorized as "social engineering." (One must presume that the "social engineering" known as the Peculiar Institution and Jim Crow needs no further action to be fully dismantled; one is invited to view the battlefield as freshly scrubbed, tabula rasa for any able-bodied, able-minded black boy or girl to leap onto, drylongso.) Most types of direct financial aid (ever shrinking over the past decade) are deemed to be "throwing money at the problem." As if the federal government were suddenly J. D. Rockefeller indiscriminately handing out shiny dimes to unwary passersby; as if buildings, job training, education, healthcare and the welfare of children—all these things—can simply take care of themselves. While, at the same time, road building, defense materiel, and agribusiness subsidies need constant tending so that their gardens might grow. This rhetoric of tough love is always presented as having the best interest of black folk at heart, but it seems rarely directed at them—Brother Fox's audience doesn't really seem to be black people, but. . .

For those of us on the ground, there appears to be a great chasm in this new Ebony Tower thinking, a wide gulf between the decrepit housing projects and the ownership of KFC Franchises, a missing link between minimum-wage jobs and paying for increasingly expensive college educations, a loose attachment—even before that promised promising education—in the very nuts and bolts of inspiring a doom-embracing generation to believe in the value of getting that education, to find a way in a world where slinging drugs and looking forward to an early, glorious death are tangible, and where medical school just seems like a fantasy.

Perhaps it is enough to sit back and blame a nine-year-old for not knowing any better, to blame his parent for not teaching him better. But blame and invective little make a cake to rise, let alone a young African American who has never heard of the College of the Holy Cross—and what it does—and who is too easily distracted by Nintendo and a cheap high and the siren song of easy money. Especially when that is the daily soundtrack of her life: hip-hop.

Hip-hop. I too distrust it. Not the music itself, but the ethos that has risen up around it and enveloped it in a shroud of bad attitude, rank materialism, disrespect, shallow boasting, superficial racial talk. Bling, bling, bitches and 'ho's; guns firing in their most Freudian sense, as well as the tiresome braggadocio regarding that real, mythic, and fleshy stand-in, that bang-bang-shoot-her-up thang in the pants. By this stage of the VIBE'd-out game, even invective against hip-hop has become a cliché.

What began as rhythmic experimentation and exaltation, grass-roots activism in the Bronx of Afrika Bambaataa and his Zulu Nation, in the smoky bars where the Last Poets performed ("Wake Up Niggers!") has metastasized into something corporate, some-thing mechanical, something over-engineered, and—perhaps most sadly—something devoid of actual relevance. The true sin of most of the hip-hop flooding today's airwaves is that it pretends to some on-the-ground connection; its most vocal proponents, and its most flashy stars, speak of its pertinence as if it were the very lifeblood of African American youth, as if it were not being largely and conspic-uously consumed by suburban white boys who've never come close to Compton or Harlem or the South Side of Chicago and who would-n't know what to do if they did; as if the music were first and fore-most about the money which too many of these "artists" merrily rap about with a bit too much wild lust; as if they had not sold their souls along with Sean "Puff Daddy/Puffy/P. Diddy/Diddy" Combs et al. (despite his admirable Voter Registration Vote-Rocking)—to some megabanker in Charlotte who couldn't care less about gangstas and pimps and gats than I do. I can only refer again to the title of the aforementioned Last Poet's song included in the soundtrack for the 1971 film *Right On!*: Wake Up!

But like every misanthrope who despises the human race yet loves his best friend, and his mama, and the cute little kid down the street, and his co-worker, and the lady at the grocery store, I adore certain acts in hip-hop and will continue to sing their praises.

Rap music, as it was originally called, began as a touchingly humble, close-to-the-ground form, a delicious, highly rhythmic, verbal percussion of self-expression that did not require the vocal instrument and training of a Billy Eckstine or an Aretha Franklin. And it could be outrageously fun ("a hip, a hop, a hippy to the hippity...") and sometimes meaningless, a true Rapper's Delight. Then came a dim time in the early 1980s when it seemed that rap music was destined to be a bygone fad of the 1970s. Yet during this time, in projects and suburbs, in basements and backyards and high school gyms and bedrooms, like an adolescent drinking his milk and taking his vitamins, rap music developed an attitude, reached backward and forward, became both world-wise and world-weary. Public Enemy taught a new generation lessons about black cultural nationalism and militant thought that might have otherwise eluded many young folk who are allergic to books. Run-DMC injected marketing smarts with new ways of merging rap with rock ("Walk this way!") in a way that no one who heard it at the time will ever forget. Rap—now officially hip-hop—was here to stay. You better make room. Artists sprang up like mushrooms. Death Row Records, Def Jam Records, and Russell Simmons seemed at one point destined to take over the world. Advertising, political campaigns, religion, and even courtrooms (See: Florida versus 2 Live Crew, circa 1992—"Nasty as You Wanna Be") all became venues for hip-hop expression, validation, amplification. Sundry forms proliferated and splintered and in turn, like a Hydra, grew new heads: speed rap, East Coast, West Coast, gangsta, horror, krunk. These days you can probably find more people who believe that Tupac is still alive than that Elvis is.

By 1999, hip-hop was being created literally all over the planet (some of the most impressive originating in Mexico, Thailand, and Egypt), and most of it was controlled by the handful of multinational corporations who had the means and motive to sell it: money honey. Nowadays, hip-hop has largely become yet another choice of soundscape for the masses to lead their lives by, another fashion choice, another song in the key of the marketplace. To be sure, individual artists of tremendous integrity and creativity and heart still play notes that resonate with the Sorrow Songs, who don't succumb to easy and denigrating stereotypes and to the wolf's howl of materialism; but, sadly they are flotsam and jetsam afloat in the mighty rushing river that carries along the rabbits and the foxes alike.

Hip-hop has been and will probably continue to be—like R&B and soul and rock 'n' roll—a uniquely American form that changed the world and the way the world looks at itself. At its best, hip-hop—when the artist, who is often composer, lyricist, and performer wrapped up in one, is not preoccupied with braggadocio and pornographic teasing, when some humanist and aesthetic agenda bubbles forth, harkens back to those early African American forms, to spirituals and gospel and most vividly the blues (ask a youngblood about Muddy Waters and he will no doubt look to the puddle at his feet, but there would be no Jay-Z or Eminem or Queen Latifah without that electrified bluesman). Don't let the blues make you bad.

Yet, certain people have a certain way of co-opting what is most genuine about hip-hop and turning it not only into stuff and nonsense, but into something quite poisonous. Exhibit A: the vast majority of hip-hop music videos and their retrograde images of half-naked women and strutting, violent, sexist, know-nothing street thugs, or fat cats gussied up to the nines, bragging about their possessions whose origins are as dim as the accompanying lyrics. ("It's all about the Benjamins...") Brother Fox with a gold grill, dripping platinum chains and drinking Cristal.

The real danger that attends the arrival of Brother Fox in the once binary white-black equation of racial relations—and he has not only arrived, but, like Daddy Mention from another tract of African American folklore, he has taken up residence in our parlor—is that he muddies the moral power of what was once unassailable. The reason we still speak of Martin Luther King, Jr., or Harriet Tubman, of Thurgood Marshall or Pauli Murray, of Frederick Douglass or Fannie Lou Hamer; the reason we, black, white, and other, still revere them, is that their march was irreducibly moral. The abolitionist movement, the civil rights movement, the Niagara movement, the Brotherhood of Sleeping Car Porters, the Freedom Riders were, at the core, moral crusades. Once the morality is removed, we are left with a not-so-easily-defined struggle. Race, as a rallying cry, as something over which to politically bond, at once loses its potency and is transformed into something unnecessary, even ugly; an excuse, something one should not be preoccupied with. ("So your skin is dark. So what?") Despite the indelible mark of history and the attendant troubles that race engenders, it becomes difficult to both define race and defend race when there is no opposition to race. And this is where race becomes a problem and not an asset. The historic freedom movements did not center on race because race in and of itself was a goodness, rather than because being Other was demonized. Once that oppositional link has been removed, what do we do with race?

The notion of color-blindness is bankrupt. Initially, the concept that a person's skin color does not matter has a certain kindergarten charm—see no evil, treat no evil. But in reality, the possibility of ever eliminating visual recognition of the Other is not only unlikely but undesirable. People want to be seen for who they are in all their complexity, their history, their baggage. To have the totality of one's self ignored is to be diminished. The problem of race is not in seeing; the problem of race is in race.

But being black is not a matter of race, ultimately. This is the queer line upon which so much foolishness proceeds: Black, Negro, African American, is not color; black is not politically created; black is not an excuse or an exception or a place to be filled. Essentially, black is a culture. To be an African American is to be part of a larger diaspora, to be linked to a once-land, a place that no longer exists, but that binds us nonetheless. Black is a learned thing. An at once fragile and strong thing. Congress can't get rid of it, and you can't buy it at Target.

Years ago, as an undergraduate, I was honored to attend a lecture by, and to meet, one of America's great historians. Benjamin Quarles was one of the founders of what we now take for granted as African American Studies. When he started, there were no African American History sections in bookstores; there weren't enough books devoted to black history to warrant such sections. He told us, that spring night, that black folk were the ur-Americans, that no group embodied the American dream as deeply and as passionately as did black folk. He told us that the Founding Fathers were smart, and that they were dreamers. They knew their designs on paper were just that: blueprints. That their Enlightenment ideals were centuries away from fulfillment. And to whom did these grand concepts matter most? Freedom. Liberty. Equality. To whom do such beliefs matter more—to the landowner or the launderer? To the colonel or the cotton picker? Blackness is not exclusive of the American Dream, it is a part of its very heartbeat. Black folk embody that dream.

For that reason an abandonment of culture becomes troublesome, somehow even sinister. This forgetfulness is the true culprit behind the rise of Brother Fox, not his craftiness—it's his shortsightedness, his selfishness. Blackness as a solely political constant denies not only history, but the reality of true freedom, true liberty, true equality, and all that those fancy—but blood-and-sweat—ideas contain. Black folk want to be free within their culture, with all the painful and glorious baggage carried along with them. Forgetting, denying, and eschewing are not true freedom, not the true American Dream. Like Gatsby, we'd be alone in our mansions, wondering who we were.

Like the best of the tricksters of old, Brother Fox should not be cast in a totally dark role. My argument is much more subtle than that. Brother Fox uses cunning in a different way than Brother Rabbit does. Self-interest is paramount, to be sure, but good can come from ambition, though it is often a by-product of that engine of personal advancement, sometimes a mask, sometimes a shield. Trust Brother Fox at your personal risk. Though only he could say, his allegiance to his kinsmen is a changeable thing, a conditional thing, a questionable thing, a malleable thing; Brother Fox can be a passionate and eloquent advocate for the Cause one minute and a most vile Judas the next. The enemy is just as easily his friend as his prey.

Curiously, almost concurrent with the aforementioned rise of the black conservative was the arrival of the black Democrat as an integral player in the system of systems that has become our government, ironically during the same time that President Reagan changed course so radically from Johnson's Great Society vision. Few people would be as important in getting William Jefferson Clinton elected as the forty-second president as was the Democratic National Committee chairman, Ron Brown, who would go on to serve as secretary of commerce. Brown was more than a figurehead. A stylish, charismatic son of upper-middle-class Harlem, a true political animal who understood the gears and levers of power from his time as a lobbyist when he came to the fore as a fundraiser and rainmaker, he represented a real shift in the diminution of race as a barrier, and the arrival of his dark-skinned brothers and sisters who came to play the government game with the rest of the kids. One might speculate that if it had not been for his untimely death in 1996 and the strange and troubling circumstances of the plane crash in which he died, which have overshadowed his career, Ron Brown might now be popularly seen as the true herald of a new order, one of greater inclusion and based more and more on meritocracy and the cool-headed reality of America's shifting demographics.

But let's be clear: Ron Brown was nobody's rabbit. He contained powerful elements of Brother Fox, down to his tailored suits and Italian loafers. But to deem Brown merely to have been a fox seems reductive, does not encompass something important, something of which he was the harbinger, something that signaled not just a change, but also an arrival.

An Ahistorical Silliness

I once heard the poet Maya Angelou declare: "I was *determined* to be brilliant." Would that it was ever so easy.

I wanted to write before I knew I wanted to write, and write I did, talking back, writing back, on paper, to Beatrix Potter, to Robert Louis Stevenson and Edgar Allan Poe and Tom Swift and the Hardy Boys. Bad poems about airplanes. A short-lived newspaper in the sixth grade, purple mimeographs ("The Indian Enterprise")—the lead article featuring quotes about the difficulties of changing back from daylight savings time. What the hell made Alexander Dumas, Charles Dickens, Victor Hugo,and Jules Vernes the heroes of a poor, illegitimate "love child" in the depths of tobacco row?

I have no idea what I looked like to the no-nonsense farmer world of Chinquapin in those Nixonian days. An annoying little semi-precocious nerd wallowing in books as if they were more than a diversion. Comic books were my original vice, and they still have more allure to me than sex or drugs. To spend too much time reading was a sign of laziness, if not worse. Decidedly evidence of bad character. Surely in my case this was true.

· · · · ·

On some very basic level I deserved it, but in many more ways no child should be subjected to such a thing by a trusted authority figure: a teacher. And though it had been designed to crush my spirit, the opposite managed to occur, aided by some angel dust and toughening familial fire.

The teacher was named Miss Underwood. Seventh-grade Social Studies. The assignment: to write a one-page personal manifesto. I think we had been studying the conquistadors or the founding of the Republic. I don't know what most of my peers wrote down that day, because the next day only two of us were asked to come to the front of the room and to read our little tracts to the class. The best paper was by a white girl who, incidentally, is still a friend, a high school teacher these days, ironically, and quite a good one. The other paper was mine.

What had I been thinking? Perhaps the words I jotted down were baldly an attempt to show off how smart I was. Perhaps I was trying to impress somebody I was sweet on. Perhaps it was just dumb. I wrote a paragraph that essentially looked down its nose at what Flannery O'Connor once called Good Country People, as if I lived on *Dynasty* with Chrystal and Blake, and summered in Hawaii with Magnum, P.I. I wrote about how *some* people didn't care about education and art and self-improvement, and how they were—figuratively of course—bound for the bad place, excommunicated, doomed. Unlike myself, who had seen the light: Hallelujah. It was full of broken sentences trying to break bad—I was thirteen—and Latinate words I'm not even certain I understood. I remember using the word *gauche*, but spelled it "gooch"—as in "Some gooch people think that their dull lives are important." Or words to that effect. In all honesty, with the perfect hindsight time gives, the hundred or so words were a rank horror. Or at least that is how I look upon them now. But they also revealed an insecurity and an unbridled ambition, a purpleness born from a need to impress and mystify, and, perhaps most obnoxious, a sense of self that did more than border on arrogance.

I read it with conviction, convinced that Tom Paine himself would weep with admiration. And—thanks to the astounding self-protection device that is early adolescence—instantly interpreted the class's guffaws and chiding as proof of their ignorance and as an underscoring of my crypto-Darwinian thesis on how some people just weren't good enough. It was a heartfelt though misguided declaration of self-help and self-empowerment, or some such, but it sounded more like Mussolini than Norman Vincent Peale, like a little black fascist in the making. (Where, how, why I held such a hatefully scornful, inaccurate, mean-spirited idea escapes me now; perhaps another defense measure to protect my fragile ego because I felt unathletic and unlovely in a world that highly prized athletics and beauty.) The din included Miss Underwood, whose baritone laughter mingled with theirs like a trombone accompanying a country-rock band.

Being so smart and so stupid at the same time is probably more blessing than curse. I rode away home that night full of righteous indignation. I had been wronged against, and some damn body would have to pay. I did not like Miss Underwood any old how. She had always treated me mean. I think I even fantasized about her losing her job over her cruel actions.

I witnessed to my ordeal before my family, testifying as I had seen others do in prayer meetings, resolute in my holy case. I produced the very document. They read it in silence, and silence remained. I waited for the vindication, for their kindred outrage, the outrage of kin, to boil forth as had mine; for them to utter condemnation's of the Wicked Witch and to vow retribution, or some such. To say, at least, that what I had written was good. Okay?

Edythe finally spoke. Edythe always terrified me. Quite simply. She was the very model of a certain Old World steadfastness that harkened back to another century. She had a way of being polished and blunt at the same time. All through my growing up I had heard tales of how as a little girl she had written a letter to the governor about a road situation, and how he stopped by to visit when he happened to be in the neighborhood, and how he fixed the problem; of how she graduated magna cum laude. I had the unshakable idea that, Urge-like, she could actually create anything, make anything happen. Later, in college, when my professor described Pope Gregory XII as so iron-willed that for him, to think of a thing was to make it so; so intense that when he walked in his garden sparks flew up from his sandals—the first image that came to my mind was of Edythe. This was not respect; this was awe.

Edythe has a way of saying my name that presages a certain level of bedrock hard-truth-telling. Equal parts maternal and prison warden. She said, "Who do you think you are?"

She reproved me for an arrogance unbecoming a thirteen-year-old, of being pretentious, of overweening ambition, of a lack of basic human decency toward other people. Who did I think I was?

They all nodded their heads in agreement. Looking at them looking at me, I could clearly read their thoughts: Where did we go wrong? My head was a puzzle, thinking that I had been doing them proud, had been upright and good and hardworking (mostly) and smart and...

What Miss Underwood had failed to achieve in public, in front of the entire class, my family had managed in their bosom.

But the most important part of this trial by class assignment had just begun. Edythe had not finished. What kind of writing is this? What is this word? We have four dictionaries in this house. *Use them.* Boy, you know verbs have to agree with their subject...

She made me rewrite the paper.

I also learned that evening—after rewriting the paper several times ("Who uses the word 'gauche'? Stop trying to impress people. What does it mean? What do you really want to say? Then say that.")—I learned that my father had killed Miss Underwood's brother.

• • • • •

When we visited my father, Harry, in prison, I had no clue as to why he had been locked up. I knew he had had a serious drug problem, and I knew, in those days, that he possessed what had been euphemistically called a Bad Attitude. Perhaps I did ask, and maybe I was told "Vehicular manslaughter," or "Shut up. None of your business." The latter was probably the case.

Truth to tell, I enjoyed the few hours' trip to Whiteville more than the awkward meeting in the prison yard—all barbed wire and hurricane fences and men (mostly black) in drab, matching duds. This did not look like the prisons I had seen on TV, and none of the men looked especially dangerous, certainly not my daddy. My grand-daddy owned a massive station wagon, which to me, at the time, could have been a ship. There was a rumble seat in back; I could have spent hours back there, oblivious to what the grown folk were talking about, watching the world recede, backwards.

Harry struck me as a nice enough fellow, a big, handsome guy with a beard upon a broad and generous face, a big gap in his front teeth so that when he smiled he made you feel good. Deep voice. He enjoyed *Gilligan's Island*, so we had something to talk about. The fact that he had a wife and a child didn't really register with me until a few years later, when I would visit them and get to know them. The connection between Harry and me I found hard to define. When my schoolmates said "My daddy," they clearly meant something different from what I meant. On the one hand there was something almost fun about having a father who could be seen as a piratical ne'er-do-well—which was how he starred in my imagination; but on the other, I understood the notion of a certain shame, but even more a regret, a loss, something broken.

That broken feeling was even more pronounced with Clara, who birthed me. Away in Brooklyn, with a husband and two children, she would write me every so often, the letters addressed to "Master Randall Garrett Dunn" (her maiden name; mine until majority). She would visit when she came down to see her family once or twice a year. I always thought she looked like Diana Ross, only better. And she seemed to have a stronger Southern accent than anyone I knew in Duplin County.

To say that our relationship was broken would be too presumptuous. It would presuppose some foundation that was never truly constructed. The older I got, the more estrangement occurred. Missed connections. Misunderstandings. Misreadings. Misfirings. Much missed. Resentment. Indifference. Many things child psychologist Melanie Klein could have a banquet delving into.

One day you look around and the world is somehow different. You have not arrived at the place you set out to achieve, and yet you have arrived somewhere, somehow. The familiar looks foreign and the foreign looks familiar. All that went before has not passed and all that is past remains. It is sentimental to think that the bits and pieces will always align; to think there is some hidden master plan. Destiny requires much more of us than simple trust. Faith is action.

Surely we are made up of all those little battles and small victories, have them at our disposal to learn from, if we so choose; and we can, if we are lucky, become better folk for the effort. Or at least that is the hope.

Years later at the Piggly Wiggly, while home on vacation, I ran into Miss Underwood by the Cap'n Crunch. She seemed positively happy to see me. She had not changed much and her voice was still clarion loud. She heaped praise upon my head like the cornucopia you see advertised at Thanksgiving time. Her sincerity was a palpable thing. She hugged me, wished me well, and requested that I stay in touch ("Don't be a stranger"), and we parted amicably. Over the years I had thought many hateful, scorn-ridden, nigh-murderous things about her. Now I felt lighter. The place where all that anger had taken up residence felt tingly and pulsed with possibility, like an old house newly renovated and painted and ready for move-in. Forgiveness seems trite to cite. As Marianne Moore once wrote: "Satisfaction is a lowly thing; how pure a thing is joy."

• • • • •

You can cry, cry, cry
I know that you know how to wail
and you can beat your head on the pavement
until the man comes and throws you in jail.

but don't let the sun catch you cryin'
cryin' round my front door

you done your baby so dirty
that's why she don't want you no more.
—"Don't Let the Sun Catch You Cryin',"
traditional blues song

"Catch the foxes for us, the little foxes that are ruining
the vineyards, While our vineyards are in blossom."
—Song of Solomon, 2:15 (NAS)

Let us be frank: We Americans currently live in a culture that praises anti-intellectualism, oddly enough. Serious thinkers don't seem to
exist in our popular media, and they are certainly not in vogue,
unless they have a gimmick, or some spectacular narrative, in which
their intellect quickly takes the back seat and is belittled. Cases-in-
point: The type of press and interest given to Stephen Hawkings
based on his Lou Gehrig's disease instead of the fact that he is one of
the most intelligent and productive thinkers ever; the fascination
over John Nash not because he is a Nobel Prize-winning mathemati-
cian who came up with ground-breaking new game theories, but
because he was unfortunate enough to suffer from a dramatic case of
schizophrenia. Pundits abound like kudzu, and are often amusing
and charming, but how often do we see award-winning anthropolo-
gists, philosophers and astrophysics involved in our daily discourse?
The Margaret Meads and Bertrand Russells and Richard Feynmans
of our era? As television critic Tom Shales once mused: Why don't
we see more smart people on TV? They would have to marry starlets
and get into drunken mischief to find the front page or the thirty-
minute omnium-gatherum we call the nightly news.

Accordingly, so much of what passes for racial discussion these days is a perpetuation of a notion of race rooted in the idea of skin color, not culture; it is superstition, not science. Race is an antique way of looking at the world involving brain size, penis size, notions of the primitive ("Soul!"), a vision cloaked in eugenics and faulty statistics (*The Bell Curve*). Negritude doesn't even begin with the color of a black person's skin; is not dictated by phenotype.

Racism is the handmaiden of race, but it proceeds from a different impulse, a different set of fairy tales. Whereas race is the definition of the Other ("You are different from me in some fundamental way"), racism is the narrative(s) woven around that assertion. Each growing on each, creating, in the mind of the teller and in the ear of the hearer and the reteller, a vision of Self based on the differentiation of the despised Other ("We do not do as they do")—and the Other is always hated for their differences, for not being Us, for having the gall to be alien, and therefore a threat. Threats exist to be feared. Hence what began as an excuse ("We can enslave them, for they are different from us") evolves, and right before the teller's eyes what was once a man transforms into a beast, as in the American South around the turn of the nineteenth century. After a series of rebellions and riots when black folk let it be known that they were not interested in remaining slaves, they became in the eyes of their masters beasts, dim-witted, childlike creatures, at once sexually rapacious and lazy; a good cook, but in desperate need of Jesus; a creature to be feared.

(Miscegenation and fear. We would do well to remember that so much of the mythical, irrational justification for racism was a fear of some big, black, well-hung beast taking advantage of a pitiful white woman. Anyone will do. Like a boy in Mississippi was feared to have done in 1955. He was only fourteen. Miscegenation is both the cause and the camouflage of the Emmett Till case. The men who murdered him probably did not fancy him some raging rapist about to grab some white woman and pleasure himself upon her. They just didn't like him. They more than didn't like him; he was to them not a boy, but an idea, a bogeyman, even at his tender age. Such a response, such a horror film-like destruction of this boy, can only be seen as a devotion to a way of seeing the world, a way of seeing the black man, no matter his age, no matter his potential danger or potential good, no matter his humanity. Fear and miscegenation.)

These dynamics are nothing new; they have been the subject of literally thousands of books, not to mention hundreds of films and television shows. And yet, in the excitement of the Information Age, most of the talk, when it comes to race, seems to be profoundly ignorant of this bedrock of American history and society, and instead clings tenaciously to fairy tales and superstitions, to silliness.

I only watched a few episodes of hip-hop-star-turned-actor-turned-producer Ice Cube's *Black. White.* The six-episode series, which aired on Rupert Murdock's FX cable network in the winter of 2005, was an update of a legendary experiment from the late 1950s, *Black Like Me.*

John Howard Griffin's 1960 memoir will remain one of the most sensational, illuminating, brave and bizarre documents of the last century. A white man who darkened his skin through a medical treatment that turned him a very dark brown, Griffin "passed" for black in the heart of the Jim Crow South—Louisiana, Mississippi, Alabama, Georgia—in 1959. The strength of the diary he kept is the continuing sense of the writer's awakening to being black in a white-supremacist society, his hypersensitivity to how he was being treated, seen, restricted. He was attendant to observations a person living a lifetime as a black person might have become inured to.

Forty-six years later we have *Black. White.* A white family, Bruno, Carmen, and their high school daughter Rose, of Santa Monica, CA, become black (cosmetically); while a black family from Atlanta—Brian, Renee and their teenaged son Nick—are made up to pass for white folk. The two families share a big Los Angeles house and the emotional sparks ensue. The white father refuses to acknowledge the existence of racism; the black father's ideas about race seem based too often on social slights; much of the show's emphasis is put on fashion and the most superficial aspects of social encounters (treatment in stores, impressions at a job interview, performing—not writing—slam poetry). The results were simply pitiful. It was as if no one in front of the camera, or behind it, had ever heard of A. Philip Randolph or Ida Wells Barnett, Sojourner Truth or Paul Laurence Dunbar, Malcolm X or Mary McLeod Bethune, Phillis Wheatley or Ralph Bunche. So many of the squabblings and misunderstandings between the two families were petty, arising from a merely surface understanding of the true cultural forces that rile "race in America" and were, most annoyingly, ahistoric. Though I'm sure the intentions of Ice Cube and his co-producers were righteous, this show was ultimately more about etiquette than about racial understanding.

To me this show does more to underscore the larger problem of the dialogue between black folks and white folks at the turn of the twenty-first century than to shed light on the true issues underlying that debate. Perhaps the fault lies in a culture that finds it difficult to have any sustained and serious discussion about anything difficult and fraught, be it death or health care or abortion. Americans love to skirt, skim the surface, raise voices and holler from a set script, for a short time, but when the topics get sticky we tend to turn the channel and leave the matter to the garbage collectors.

The entire idea of racial profiling, of snap judgments based on what the eye can see, has been (or at least should be) turned on its head in the peculiar and harsh light that has shone on us in the hours and weeks and years since the September 11th strike on America. Can you pick out an Arab by sight? Do most Americans know the difference between a Persian and a Turk? What does a Christian Lebanese look like? There have existed black Arabs for more than a millennium. Can we visually differentiate between a Sunni and a Wahhabi, a Bohra or a Druze?

These days what do we talk about, truly, when we talk about race? Silly White Person says to Silly Black Person: "You are black because you have dark skin. Forget about your skin and you shall be as me." Silly Black Person says to Silly White Person: "My skin is my identity; the sum of my being is bound up with you, White

Person, discriminating against me." These exchanges happen daily over the airwaves—without a sense of history, petty, thin, superficial—and they leave one to assume that such exchanges are occurring on the street, in the workplace, and in the lobbies of movie theaters. Negritude doesn't even begin with the color of a black person's skin, nor does it vanish when opposition fades.

Once upon a time, not too very long ago, the debate, the talk, the discussion about race was much more visceral, became physical at times, had more at stake—actually had the ability to change lives. It was not a kaffeeklatsch, not a "gotcha" game of who called whom what at some celebrity party or behind the stage last night at some awards show; it was a roiling, heartfelt, national tussle: People actually wanted to get somewhere. Somewhere new. Somewhere better.

· · · · ·

Who named boxing the Sweet Science?

Apparently the writer A. J. Liebling took it (he published a collection of essays called *The Sweet Science* in 1956) from an eighteenth-century text by Pierce Egan, *Boxiana*. "The Sweet Science of Bruising" is how he phrased it.

Bruising indeed. I freely admit that I have only tried it one and a half times, and I can testify that one truly does see stars when using one's head to stop an accelerating fist clothed in a leather glove. All our myths, all our dreams, all our fantasies, all our insecurities, all our narrative urges, all our wretchedness is bound up in boxing. The history of our country for the last two centuries features boxing in such a way as to appeal to our waking dreams. A phallocentric exaltation of masculinity, unapologetic and delicious in its bloody glory. Even as we feign disgust at the brutality, we seem to cherish the purity of the violent display and what lies underneath: something ancient and deeply human. We trot out stories about boxing when we are feeling pugnacious, or when we are sentimental about our will to power, our collective ability to overcome. Paintings, sculptures, movies, short stories, novels, even poems about boxing have poured forth like a mighty stream through our American musing about ourselves, our victory of the will.

All sport functions in a similar way: as ritualized battle, a way to fight and die and be reborn to fight again. We identify vicariously with one football team, one tennis player, one golfer. They become our champion. Champions have always functioned as more than mere entertainment, more than a diversion on a Sunday afternoon—too much meaning becomes attached to them. We invest them with something spiritual. Something primal. The madding soccer mobs aren't simply blowing off steam when they riot. Boxers, however, are at once more elegant and more powerful than most sports figures. Their individuality and the nature of their conflict—their physiques, their focus, their personal history—is somehow simply poetic. The stuff of epics.

Very early in the twentieth century—in fact going back to the post-Civil War years, when boxing was nothing more than brawling at the county fair—African Americans found in the sport a metaphor; something even more than a physical manifestation of power; expression, vindication, triumph, something that embodied a destiny, an existential passion play, a prophesy of their place in American society ("The champion of the world is a black man!"). No one galvanized that narrative power more than Jack Johnson, the first black boxing king, who won the heavyweight title in 1908 after years of being refused an opportunity to fight the white champions. Audacious even in death, he treated the onlooking world to a type of Bad Negro: arrogant, moneyed, physically unbeatable, nonchalant—even defiant—in his consorting with white women, unbowed before authority.

("That Jackson Johnson is a big, strong, burly, rough darkey, I'll admit, and being champion of the world he may feel that he has a perfect right to run over, beat up, ignore and otherwise make life miserable for others, but he should not forget that Samson ruled the world with all his strength, but his love for a woman got him killed." Uncle Rad Kees, Indianapolis *Freeman*.)

Johnson emboldened and lifted up the public morale of the rank and file of Black America for a time, and he inspired such ire among the white populace to conjure up the idea of the Great White Hope. ("JACK JOHNSON IS CRUCIFIED FOR HIS RACE. FAMOUS FISTIC GLADIATOR SAILS FOR FRANCE AFTER BEING PERSECUTED IN THE UNITED STATES. WHAT HAS HE DONE?" Chicago *Defender*.) The drama of his life, something akin to a Greek tragedy interspersed with comedy, is both inspiring and a cautionary tale; it reveals much about how deeply race is woven into the fabric of the American story. The way Johnson toyed with police and governments over his gambling, his choice of women, his outspokenness, rings louder than that of any sport. The life, the event, of Jack Johnson is not only a metaphor for the African in America in the early part of the twentieth century, but also the substance of things hoped for and the evidence of things yet to come.

Perhaps that explains the temptation to look upon the history of African American boxers as some sort of road map, some series of battles through which the Freedom Movement and the charts of black folks' lives can be interpreted. These men have become symbols and we try to make them more.

From Joe Louis, who was the antithesis of Johnson, as if he had gazed upon his titanic forebear and attempted to do everything opposite—except that he still won fights. Where Johnson was arrogant, Louis was humble; where Johnson was a spendthrift, he was frugal and enterprising; where Johnson was a philanderer and womanizer and miscegenationist, he was faithful to his black wife; where Johnson was a gambler and good-time dandy, he was a churchgoing model of rectitude. Joe Louis held the heavyweight title for eleven years, including through World War II, and his most famous, indeed legendary, fight was against the German, Nazi-affiliated Max Schmeling, a curious Great White Hope indeed, in a pitched battle laden with propaganda and awkward, even prescient American pride, especially among the African American community.

In Floyd Patterson, in Sonny Liston, more icons emerged, but then along came Cassius Clay, a good-looking, silver-tongued, seemingly unstoppable fighter, who would dominate the sport the way none other had dominated any sport: The Greatest of All Time, as he liked to say. Moreover, the soon-renamed Muhammad Ali seemed to embody his era with almost Biblical/Koranic flair—going to jail as a conscientious objector, becoming a fixture in the civil-rights movement, he bridged the gap from sit-ins and boycotts to entering the boardrooms and lecture halls and sitting anywhere on the bus black folk damn well felt like sitting.

It is very tempting to use these icons as signposts, as talismans. For, after his successive losses and returns and ultimate retirement and descent into illness, despite the ring being crowded with foxlike, goatlike pretenders—a churlish George Foreman, an irascible Joe Frazier, a clownish Leon Spinks—Ali reigns in the hearts of Americans, of the world.

What then do we make of the less inspiring though no less supremely athletic Evander Holyfield? Of the diasporic wonder of the magnificent Lennox Lewis? And of the terror who is Mike Tyson? All these men are without a doubt phenomenal athletes, and arrived at the top of the heap by den of their will and discipline and intelligence and bodies, but none have captured the world's imagination in any way resembling the way Ali has done; none have achieved that metaphorical leap Jack Johnson or Joe Lewis enjoyed, becoming indispensable parts of African American mythology. Has boxing's importance declined so sharply in so short a time? Is it the sport, the athletes, or the people? Sports figures and sports still hold a major sway over a huge swath of America, but the once symbolic power of the boxer to inspire across a number of stories seems to have dimmed. Omens of tribulations to come, perhaps? Or a sign of a certain creeping rot? Or of the ultimate failure of the Cult of Personality to do more than inspire? A limit in the ability of one life's narrative to fully contain all the answers to so complex, so damnable a problem as Race in America?

I think George Foreman's later public incarnation(s) simply perplexed Mr. Brown, the former boxer and boxing trainer, still in love with the sport, shouting instructions from his armchair to the fighters on TV. He would watch the former terror, now all soft and cuddly and smiling like a Teddy bear as he hawked kitchen appliances. Mr. Brown was clearly bemused by Foreman's paradoxical rise and fall and rise to the overweight fortysomething making a fool of himself in the ring for money; to the preacher with five sons all named George; to the gazillionaire salesman of mufflers and an eponymous grill for fat-free cooking. When Mr. Brown's daughter gave me one of those machines for Christmas, he looked upon it as if it were radioactive. It was as if commercial success had somehow tainted another, more exalted, once-glory. Here was a man once so full of Hell that even Satan would have been afraid to go toe-to-toe with him. We remember those indelible images of him in Kinshasa just before the famous Zaire Rumble in the Jungle, under the Midas glare of the truly Satanic Mobutu Sese Seko Kuku Ngbendu wa za Banga, with big, tall, titanic Foreman barely verbal, full of an unspeakable and unknown bitterness and a volcanic spite I'm sure he tapped to fuel his bulging musculature.

And yet there is something quintessentially American about the many transformations of George Foreman, especially the canned exuberance he would eventually bring to his role as salesman. He dials an entirely different frequency to wild-haired, legally-challenged, slantwise-wordsmith, boxing promoter Don King's well-worn phrase: Only in America. Maybe, in many ways, they are the two most apt symbols to chime with the current state of Black America, making friends with the marketplace, an uneasy new comfort with a truly colorless bottom line.

O ye wicked generation, looking for a sign! To be sure, one can't help but be tempted to make hay of such an impressive list of black heavyweight champions; to take the careers of these latter-day gladiators and read them like a soothsayer reading auguries in the entrails of a slain goat. Tempting because we have used them as symbols for so long, sometimes to great avail, sometimes to our detriment. But you can't Rope-a-Dope history. You can try for a spell, but sooner or later even the best will run out of gas. Our arms are too short to box with destiny; we must learn to dance with it.

> "Life is like boxing in many unsettling respects. But boxing is only like boxing."
> —Joyce Carol Oates

• • • • •

"Niggah, please!"

When I was a boy, my two best buddies in the whole entire wide world were my cousins, the identical twins Harry and Larry. Six years my senior, they treated me like a younger brother and I was as slavishly devoted to them as a puppy. Along with them I would witness—and get involved in—boyfull mischief that I was either too ignorant or too timid to attempt on my own. They took me riding on their minibikes. They took me along to dogfights. We snuck into places we had no business being in. They took me to swimming holes where they skinny-dipped and (once) fled from alligators. When I was old enough, they took me to my first juke joint. Any trouble available to rambunctious youths in Chinquapin, in our little tract of Duplin County (which, in hindsight, is a pretty small territory and about as tame as it gets) was their province. As the sons of an elementary-schoolteacher mother and a high-school-teacher and church-deacon father, they took as their mandate pulling on trouble's braids. I had a fantastic time being their mascot.

Among the tomfoolery in which they engaged was taking me to R-rated movies (I think for a brief time they too were under-aged—even more the fun). There were only two theaters in Duplin County at the time (now there are none). One was a rickety drive-in in Beulaville. The other was a proper theater in Wallace. This was in the early 1970s and the heyday of so-called blaxploitation pictures. Harry and Larry were particularly fond of Rudy Ray Moore movies—*Dolemite*, with Moore tooling around in his great big Cadillac, dressed in the most outrageous pimp style, loud and obnoxious and obscene. Not the proudest moment in African American comedy, but he probably holds a special place among the raunchiest, most off-color, and most sexually outrageous comedians of them all.

Of these days, one moment sticks in my mind—during those many viewings of *Truck Turner* and *Enter the Dragon* and *Abby* and *Blackenstein* and *Walking Tall* and *Shaft in Africa*—in 1973, while seeing *The Exorcist*. I was ten, and I know now that the experience marked me for life. (In fact, my first novel was about demon possession, although I only made the *Exorcist* connection years after the book was published.)

Most of the time, the audience in Wallace was practically 100 percent black. Early on in the movie, a gentlemen a few rows in front of us commenced to heckle. He found the movie a bit dull. "This shit ain't scary. I thought this was supposed to be a scary pitcher. I want my money back. Who gives a shit about this little white bitch?"

The movie progressed. Clearly something was amiss with little Regan. When Linda Blair's chalky head spun around and the distinctive voice of Mercedes McCambridge croaked out, our heckling friend fled the theater. Larry (or was it Harry?) made note of the exit: "Bet that nigger's scared now!" The entire audience erupted in hoots and howls—at the scariest part of the movie.

I sing not only of horror flicks, but of Negroes' seeming affection for the word "nigger."

• • • • •

In 2002, the Harvard law professor Randall Kennedy published *Nigger: The Strange Career of a Troublesome Word* (which should not be confused with Dick Gregory's classic 1964 autobiography, *Nigger.*) A short book about a heavy topic. Neither proscriptive nor condoning,

Professor Kennedy's agenda is to simply put the word in context historically and legally, something rarely done when it comes to the more inflammatory racial thinking. The book created a firestorm, not least by entertaining the idea that there might a legitimate place for the word amongst those who use it most these days: black people. Kennedy takes us back to the origin of the word, which was merely descriptive at first, and did not become derogatory until the 1830s when it became an intentional insult and much, much more. Throughout the nineteenth century, the meaning of the word "nigger" was unambiguous and accompanied by a threat and some of the worst examples of man's inhumanity to man in recorded history.

But sometime in the early twentieth century, long before Jim Crow had been plucked and cooked, as an autonomous black culture, both down on the farm and up in the urban rainforests, arose and took pride in itself, the use of the infamous word took on new timbres. Make no mistake: Black people were still being lynched, redlined to their side of town, kept out of major universities, barred from voting; the meaning and sting and censoriousness of the word were still very much in effect. But "nigger" among the niggers was increasingly becoming a plastic word, something malleable, useable, manipulable; its poison could be leached out and the vessel, those six letters, used for other work. The matter was never so simple as simply turning the word on its head and making what had been bad into what was now good. Many black people who employed the word toward other black people meant it in as wicked a sense as did the most committed Klu Klux Klan member. Yet a multiplicity of meanings emerged, an array of uses, a variety of notes could be played with it. Among the works of the Harlem Renaissance writers are some of the most artful uses of the word—as weapon, as balm, as catnip, as Spanish Fly. (Carl van Vechten, a dear white friend of both Zora Neale Hurston—who herself wielded the word like a hatchet in one hand and like a posey in the other—and Langston Hughes, wrote a novel, *Nigger Heaven*, that was much lauded by the niggerati (Hurston's coinage).)

By the 1960s and the Black Power movement, the word was a birdie on a badminton court. Black Panthers, hippies, crackers, governors, some Black Muslims, Pullman car porters, and maids used the word liberally and with moxie, both against and in the service of black people. But never was it so acrobatically bandied about than during that earlier-mentioned, bizarre yet delicious period of celluloid during the 1970s, ushered in by Melvin Van Peebles' outrageous, obscene, militant, empowering, and industry-changing *Sweet Sweetback's Baadasssss Song*. Characters like Shaft, Black Caesar, Superfly, Cleopatra Jones, Truck Turner, Dolemite, and a peanut gallery of dark faces let fly with enough "niggers" to sink an armada. I look back on those films with mixed feelings, but largely with a sense of nostalgia and glee. Even as a child I was aware of the complexity inherent in the use of the word; I had some glimmer of understanding of the depth of its history, and also a distinct and personal identification with the word when it was used as a term of endearment or a clever tool for self-mockery.

I was a college student in 1982, the year Richard Pryor released the concert film *Live on the Sunset Strip*. This was his first film since his ill-fated freebasing accident of a few years before. Pryor had been, and still is, acknowledged as the King of Comedy, the one after whom everything changed. He had squeezed more juice out of a single word than a Minute Maid factory could from an entire Florida of orange groves, more than anyone in the long line of comics going back to the first black minstrels, vaudeville, the Chitlin Circuit, and Amos 'n' Andy ever had before.

But now, in 1982, Richard told us, after a trip to Africa, after nearly meeting his maker, after seeing the beauty of the West African people (who looked so much like people back home), that he had seen the error of his ways and that he was never ever going to use the word "nigger" again. (Curiously enough, that same year, an album of his "greatest hits" hit the stands—*Supernigger*. Maybe the record company had other ideas.)

I had gone to see the movie on a Saturday night with a group of folk including a good buddy also named Richard, and we talked about the word and Pryor's decision long into the night after the show. I had adored Richard Pryor from my time as a cub and continued to adore him, even if I disagreed with his self-censorship. At nineteen I fretted over what I saw as a largely superficial, even sentimental response to the magnitude of the African diaspora: Black folk are indeed larger than the Middle Passage, and to encounter the vastness of what slavery has wrought—from the West Indies to the Americas to the source of our legacy—is to be shocked, humbled, uplifted, chastened even. But did Pryor really just reach this insight at the age of forty-one? Should we look back upon all his riotous riffs, his cleverness, his genius, with a jaundiced eye? All that wordplay? All those times he had unfurled the word "nigger" as if it were

Superman's cape? Used it as a knife to White America's carotid artery? Or as a multicolored quilt, stained with blood and warmed with a mother's love to swaddle a homeboy? Can the massive frigates of history so easily be turned about? Are words so fixed in their original meanings that they cannot be reappropriated, recharged, resurrected, born again?

Some would have us believe that the word is so blood-soaked, so scornful, such a thing-maker, that to breathe it is to make a thing out of yourself, to unwittingly buy into the overarching, all-powerful worldview of White Supremacy.

Nigger, please.

My friend Richard said he could see both sides. He said he was going to take the matter under advisement.

I knew even then that the use of the word nigger was much more complex that what Mr. Pryor had reduced it to. By denying that the history the word had among black folk—the history it had with him—he lost sight of the true genius of black people. For me, when my lover or my brother or my mother calls me "My nigger," I know exactly what they mean, and it vibrates on levels undreamt of by people who would deny me my humanity.

Meanwhile, in the well-heeled suburbs of Scottsdale and San Diego, Shaker Heights and Scarsdale, any one of us can find a rich white boy who would take it as the highest honor on Earth for you—with great sincerity and at the top of your voice—to greet him as "Nigger."

For some these ideas are abhorrent; for them the word is fixed, eternally, in the actions and mindset of the enemy; for them language is more powerful than the user. But for me the amazing thing is that the word can still be used as a sword. At the end of the day it really is just a word, children. Like "ox" and "sin" and "fear" and "hate" and "catsup" and "peanut butter." We use language; language does not use us. If, however, the whirligig of talk spins the other way around, you have larger, more pressing problems. Better to worry about sticks and stones, hedge funds and mortgage rates, voter-registration reform and unemployment. Those are the things that can break your bones and hurt you.

As time marched on and the entire American populace—not just the liberals—became more politically correct (i.e., polite), the word suddenly became much more dangerous than it had been even in the '50s or '60s or '70s—the huge irony being that in 1950 if you were black and someone called you "nigger," you were probably in certain peril, one way or the other. If, in the Internet Age, you are black and someone calls you "nigger," he or she is (a) deranged, (b) masochistic, (c) another black person, or (d) a white person trying desperately to be hip.

At the center of this emblematic difference of viewpoint within the black community, so many years after slavery has ended, with segregation largely squelched, and in a time when we have ourselves an Oprah Winfrey and a Condi Rice—at the center rests a disagreement about the meaning of blackness. Though I, like my friend Richard, could always see both sides, the argument always seemed weaker than water to me.

The work needing to be done is much deeper than epithets and good manners. The roots of the problems lie in a mutual not-knowing, a mutual belief in Otherness, a reluctance to give voice to deeper mistrusts. In order to bridge that gap, bit by bit, brick by brick, we must dismantle the House of Race. It is not a word; it is a way of thinking. It is not a white thing, or a black thing; it is an American thing.

Ethnicity, yes; race, forget about it. This shift will continue to be a tricky business, but our changing demographics make the shift not only inevitable but centrally important. It is not difficult to understand that many Americans are sentimental about race, perhaps none more so than Brother Rabbit. The great fear is that by deemphasizing race, not only will identity be lost, but some collective power; and that ancestors will be dishonored or betrayed. Regardless of those misgivings, that great work is already afoot.

Who was it who said that there is nothing more irresistible than an idea whose time has come?

•••••

I remember with great fondness the much-beloved and highly sentimental 1971 made-for-television movie *Brian's Song*, with its soaring music ("The Hands of Time") that can still be heard via Muzak in elevators around the world. The film is mawkish without shame: Only under the rubric of sports do you see American alpha males allow themselves to be so tender; to blubber freely and be applauded for it. Only in sports is it okay for big, strong he-men to be sentimental. Based on Gayle Sayers' best-selling memoir *I Am Third*, the movie is an account of the African American football player's friendship with his fellow Chicago Bear, Brian Piccolo, and of Piccolo's death from cancer at age twenty-seven. There is a memorable scene in which Sayers (Billy Dee Williams) and Piccolo (James Caan) are exercising and bonding. At one point, Piccolo, in a moment of mock fury, calls Sayers a nigger. They both collapse into paroxysms of laughter. It is an unforgettable scene, centuries of history and future collapsed into one indelible moment, a recognition of the folly, a leap in openness and vulnerability, an acknowledgment of these two men's fixed realities (in the 1960s) and of their love for each another. It is one of those unusual, raw, true glimpses, amidst the vast detritus of mass media, of humanity and friendship and truth. Today, despite all the *Lethal Weapon*s and *Rush Hour*s and *Die Hard*s and all the other buddy-buddy black-and-white, black-and-Asian, and whatever other mixture action pictures, depictions of such genuine and telling interactions remain rare, are hardly ever captured and laid before the masses. You won't see such a thing on broadcast television today, and probably not on cable either.

• • • • •

Mr. John W. Brown lost his eyesight just before he died. I think we refused to admit it; he admitted to some difficulty in seeing, but he managed to get around and even sat before the television, only asking now and again for us to tell him about what was going on. But once he was in the hospital, a note over his bed read *Patient is blind*. Many illusions began to fade with that, along with a certain degree of magical thinking.

He suffered from a rare vascular disorder. It had originally stricken him fourteen years before, and had actually killed him, clinically. But he had been revived and, in the fullness of time, he regained almost full health, save the loss of a thumb due to the vascular damage.

The loss of eyesight had been particularly galling, for Mr. Brown had been an avid reader. If my bookishness had struck most of the community as queer and a waste of time, I could always rely on him as a champion. Always each day began with the newspaper and a prolonged discussion about those idiots in Washington. I had delighted so much in his delight in the novel *Jaws* and sharks that in later years I would try to find more books for him featuring sharks. And books about sports figures. I remember his relish of a biography of Jackie Robinson that his daughter had given him for Christmas. The ensuing lectures about Robinson (whom he had seen from the stands), about segregation, about the dignity and symbolism and responsibility of black athletes, could literally go on for hours.

His eyesight had been threatened once before, but in a different way.

That early spring, when the Pile was almost worn down. By this time I knew it would soon be history. Had it been possible, I would have been out there that day alongside Mr. Brown, digging, chopping, burning. I loved the smell of the many fires he kept burning to get rid of the debris.

He was alone when the thorn from a bush caught his eye. The cut was deep. A true puncture. So deep in fact that the vitreous fluid quickly drained out. The eye collapsed. Edythe rushed him to the hospital in Kinston. Who knew that, if properly stitched, an eyeball will reinflate like a beach ball?

The eye patch made him look very like a pirate (my boyhood obsession), and he joked about the entire affair, but it was tinged with gravitas. No one wants to lose an eye.

Soon he was back to work.

As simple as it seems, it's all about learning how to see.

There Is a River

Listening for God's Trombones: The Black Church Now

For the student of American history, in the face of our current climate of religious debate—now archly conservative, now Fundamentalist-fired—it must seem odd that, for most of the twentieth century, when religion and politics met the combination has tended to yield a left-wing firebrand. Think Reinhold Niebuhr, a critic of labor exploitation and an ardent pacifist; think Dorothy Day, a founder of *The Catholic Worker*, devoted to the downtrodden and a worker among the urban poor; think Aimee Semple McPherson, the first truly major broadcast evangelist, a white woman who dared venture into the segregated South and preach to all colors and creeds and invite them into her extravaganza of worship ("The Four Square Gospel"). These Christian soldiers took their marching orders from Jesus's philosophy of love and from the Holy Spirit: "Greater love hath no man than this, that a man lay down his life for his friends" (John 15:13). Quick to criticize the Establishment in all its earthly power, they cast their lots with the humblest, with the neediest, with society's most wronged.

Since before Emancipation, the Black Church had always kept those ideals front and center. From the Abolitionists who founded the African Methodist Episcopal Church in 1787, to the free-food-giving Sweet Daddy Grace in the early 1900s with his Pentecostal United House of Prayer for All People, to Father (General Jealous) Divine ("*Peace* is truly wonderful!") and his Harlem-based International Peace Movement of the 1930s—the linchpins of the African American Church have always been uplift, community, the care and upkeep of the soul, and a loud voice against injustice.

"God's Trombones," James Weldon Johnson once called them, the eloquent, forceful, moral leaders from the pulpits with their home-grown, Biblically based rhetoric ("And God, sitting high up in his Heaven / Laughed at poor Pharaoh.") Theirs was not an institution overly concerned with legalistic interpretations of Scripture, or quick to censure and cast out; not an institution in love with power and involving itself with the packing of courts, with recasting American History in some artificially sanitized image and demonizing anyone who disagreed with their worldview; not an institution bent on imposing a narrow and exclusive set of moral dicta, and invading every bedroom and telecast and strip club.

The pulpit conveys a palpable authority, easily used, abused, misused, or benignly neglected, and it can sometimes camouflage a multitude of sins. When used as a tool of righteousness, the pulpit can be a nearly irresistible force. These men (and they were almost all men in those days) were not perfect, but surely a Martin Luther King, Jr., was preordained by history, a brilliant trumpet sounding in chorus with an ancestral brass section, part of a true American tradition, established among the Quaker abolitionists and the missionaries abroad and at home, in the slave uprisings whose leaders invoked Moses and Joseph and the intemperate, righteous anger of King David, God's Beloved; surely they too were anointed young men, Methodist, Baptist, Catholic, et al., who set out among the carpetbaggers, through the Reconstructing South, to establish, tiny flock by tiny flock, the foundation upon which a great edifice would rise within less than a century, whose authority was unimpeachable and where ministers, faulty human beings all, often, somehow, managed to walk on water nonetheless.

In such light the question looms: Where is the Black Church now? One need not look too hard to find a black minister bemoaning the shrinking congregations on Sunday mornings, the diminished funding and vanishing structure. Where is that clarion voice that issued from the battlements of power and called them to task? Where are the Jesus-inspired troubadours in the projects and sweatshops and hospitals?

A case in point might be an ongoing and worsening current problem: AIDS. How would the Black Church of old, at its most energized, most inclusive, most active, have dealt with the current pandemic? A scourge that is devastating poor black women and young black men with the rapaciousness of a chimera on the loose. Despite the fickle American media's approach to the subject, HIV/AIDS continues to be a major threat to people the world over, including in the U.S., and especially among black folk. Perhaps the virus carries with it too much taint of the flesh (sin) and was stigmatized early as a Plague of Judgment, or perhaps the present-day Black Church sees its work as being elsewhere, but the absence of its voice and leadership is conspicuous in the light of history.

That silence is just one of the ways the traditional African American church seems to some observers to be eroding. Perhaps we should weep and sing a requiem for the once-powerful Black Church, once seen the world over as a beacon of righteousness. But would that dirge be sung too soon?

Perhaps so, for an interesting change has been working, not in an alleyway, but right before our eyes. The manifestation has taken another form, not that of a traditional white-steeple congregation, but more in tune with our present-day digital age. Before we write off the Black Church as a thing of the past, have a care:

When President George W. Bush made one of his belated visits to devastated New Orleans and the Gulf Coast in late 2005, he showed unusual sensitivity by walking flanked by the virile-looking though embattled Mayor Ray Nagin and the gargantuan and commanding figure of the Reverend T. D. Jakes. The mega-pastor's presence seemed like a last-minute, self-protective move by the forty-third president—who had seemed to have little use for the black clergy—but it was a wise choice nonetheless, for Jakes represents the new wave of Black Christendom and an important new direction.

An orator of no mean talents, Pastor Jakes holds his own among the new breed of megachurch mega-pastors, the Rick Warrens (Saddleback Church) and Joel Osteens (Lakewood Church), who count their congregations in the tens of thousands and whose television shows reach many millions of viewers. Jakes' Dallas-based Potter's House Church has a congregation the size of a small city, and its annual MegaFest draws more than 100,000 people. The ministry produces movies and recordings and all the other requisite postmodern media platforms that a postmodern congregation requires, from daily shows on several networks to gospel CDs to Web pages and podcasts.

Critics of these newfangled megalopolises of Christ point out the inward thrust of most of these ministries, the thrust toward a capitalist-friendly message tailored to the hearts and minds of the new middle classes. These pastors don't exactly say "Greed is good," but they don't preach the centuries-old warning: "And again I say unto you, It is easier for a camel to go through the eye of a needle, than for a rich man to enter into the kingdom of God" (Matthew 19:24). God, these new telegenic ministers say, does not want you to be poor.

But where some see cynical, media-savvy marketeers, others see positive forces of personal uplift with literally millions of personal stories of deliverance from empty, directionless lives; from drugs and other addictions. Where some see an insular world of self-help and obsession with self-esteem, others point toward charity and outreach befitting a world so chaotic and wide that a door-to-door approach has become an ineffectual thing of the past.

That said, let us not forget:

Dexter Avenue Baptist Church. Montgomery, Alabama. Vernon Johns is an object lesson when it comes to too-early condemnation, counting-out, scorn for and dismissal of the potential promise of the Black Church and its future. Johns was and is an American original whose story is nowhere nearly as well known as it should be. Born in rural Virginia in 1892, the son of farmers who were too poor to send him to school, he is said to have taught himself Latin, Greek, Hebrew, and German. He possessed a photographic memory, we are told in perhaps the best account of his life, Taylor Branch's prize-winning *Parting the Waters*. Having finally found a way into schools in Virginia, he eventually transferred to Oberlin College, from which he graduated with honors. Years of colorful teaching and preaching throughout the South followed, and Johns gained a reputation as a brilliant orator and writer, and for literally working his land and entering the pulpit covered in dirt. At one point he worked as a fishmonger: "I don't apologize for it, because for every time I got one call about religion, I got forty calls about fish." Early on, his rhetoric was exceptional not only for its erudition, but because of his passionate crusade for racial justice. He was not a man of compromise or gingerly diplomacy.

In 1947, a well-heeled church in Alabama took him on as its pastor. He preached what were considered to be inflammatory sermons ("It's Safe to Murder Negroes in Montgomery") and called for boycotts and other forms of civil disobedience. This behavior did not sit well with the pillars of the prestigious church. He was a rabble-rouser and a boat-rocker, not a gentleman. He might be brilliant, but he did not go down well on Sunday mornings or any other day of the week. He had the nerve to sell his farm produce at the church. He would order food in the white section of restaurants. Not the done thing. So, in 1953, after six years, he was let go.

The next minister that the Dexter Avenue Baptist Church hired was an up-and-comer. A bright young scion of a high-toned Atlanta family whose father was pastor of one of the Black Middle Class' most elite churches. A Morehouse College graduate. Soon to have a PhD in Systematic Theology from Boston University. Dashing, handsome, elegant. Surely the Reverend Martin Luther King, Jr., would know how to behave himself among good people. Then along came Mrs. Rosa Parks. Just the right spark. . .

One of the many ironies of this story is that King would lead the conservative-with-a-small-"c" congregation into the nation's most emblematic acts of civil disobedience and catapult the entire nation into a civil-rights movement that would be known the world over and ultimately shift the course of a great nation. Another is that the Reverend Vernon Johns would go on to mentor other ministers who would form the Southern Leadership Conference. King himself, near the end of his life, would turn to Johns' own work for inspiration.

King's wonderfully effective speech before the strikers in Memphis, Tennessee, on March 18, 1968, was modeled on a sermon Johns wrote in 1949, "Segregation After Death": "Dives went to hell because he allowed Lazarus to become invisible. Dives went to hell because he allowed the means by which he lived to outdistance the ends for which he lived. Dives went to hell because he maximized the minimum and minimized the maximum.... And I come by here to say that America too is going to hell if she doesn't use her wealth."

Sometimes a great ship can be righted. Sometimes. . .

Even more important to remember: Those same members of Dexter Avenue Baptist Church were ultimately the people who made the famous boycott work. The same doctors and lawyers and dentists and cabdrivers and schoolteachers who had found the Reverend Johns too much to take found within themselves the courage to stand up in the storm.

The Fruit of Islam

"Islam" means "peace" in Arabic. It is important to remember this.

But some will say that "Islam" means "submit," as in submission to God, Allah. Some say it means "love." Ultimately, as in all text-based religions, the argument comes down to semantics—but semantics, being about words, comes down to interpretation. In either case, to look upon Islam and not consider it to be, objectively, one of the Earth's most beautiful religions is to be tone-deaf. A cousin to Christianity and Judaism with more than one billion adherents, book-based, historically colorful and significant, spiritually self-effacing, both inward- and outward looking, altruistic and centered around love—this religion should not be foreign to Americans. Yet it both is and it is not.

Legend has it that Elijah Poole met Wallace Fard Muhammad in 1931, a year after WFM had founded the Nation of Islam, a curious mingling of ancient Islamic theology with homespun myth and racial politics. Poole became the founder's right hand and successor and ultimately the Honorable Elijah Muhammad, and one of America's most influential leaders, whether the gatekeepers of official U.S. history wish to admit him or not. The theology of the Nation of Islam is difficult for me to fully apprehend. It mixes much of Christianity and Sufism and Judaic tradition as well as Egyptian lore and Great Depression populist race talk and some stuff that is clearly just made up—yet its followers are sincere and serious and deserving of a degree of respect if for nothing else but their stalwart and admirable discipline. To be sure, the Honorable Elijah Mohammad's reaction to the state of Black America in his time was not unlike that of scores of other contemporary movements and large numbers of everyday black folk meeting a white-supremacist, lynch-happy ethos with scorn and distrust. What now appears as simply racist—the unabashed hatred of white people, the mythology of white folk as the authors of all evil in the world, etc., and was not singular to him—it was a full-fledged survival doctrine at the time. Some of his contemporaries embraced Communism as an antidote, while others, like Marcus Garvey, led movements of repatriation to Africa. Yet the paradox, as with so much of so many home-grown American religions, is how much good the Nation of Islam has accomplished, especially among the least considered of African

Americans: young black men. Prisons, in particular, became fecund ground for Muhammad's message, as much for its appeal for self-realization as for its unapologetic hatred of the descendants of Europeans (whether their ancestors were enslavers or not) and for an ill-advised anti-Semitism.

Yet this was the creed that initially captured the rage and energy that would inspire Malcolm X, formerly Detroit Red, formerly Malcolm Little, and ultimately Al-Hajj Malik El-Shabazz: his very nomenclature illustrates the American journey of identity writ small.

El-Shabazz's famous discovery of the true message of Islam, his break with the Honorable Elijah Muhammad and the subsequent tragedy of his assassination in 1965, cannot be put aside when one considers the legacy of the Nation of Islam. We would be remiss in dismissing the positive impact the organization has had on generations of black men and women. The empowerment, the beachhead the Nation has formed within prison communities—a world nearly abandoned in American culture as their ranks continue to swell with African American men (approaching one million at this writing)—the physical and entrepreneurial infrastructure that its temples and publications and businesses have engendered. And despite what one thinks of Louis Farrakhan, the Nation of Islam's leader now for many decades, whose succession to the seat held by the Honorable Elijah Muhammad was once disputed, who, despite his violin virtuosity, is no Teddy bear, with his Million Man Marches and his latter-day rhetoric designed to inflame white folks, Jewish folk, even many black folk—the home-grown Nation of Islam cannot be blotted out of American history and must be given its rightful place among the other American-born religious institutions in all their problematic and singular realities—felicitous, bizarre, antagonistic, disputatious, inventive, investing. But it has made perceptions even more problematic for black American Muslims who align themselves, as did El-Shabazz finally, with the more traditional form of Islam. Since the fateful bombings in September of 2001, a curious silence has fallen over American followers of that religion. The media has seemed to largely abandon any discussion of the tangled relationship between the Nation of Islam and traditional Islam, with the decades-long involvement of generations of Americans with Islam. How odd, since in many ways those questions may hold a vital key to unlocking the current unpleasantness that seems to overwhelm the world in a Holy War, as sect battles sect, as fundamentalism displaces free-flowing thought and exchange, as roots of hatred threaten to choke off the taproot of love and brotherhood.

Or perhaps when, after the assassination of President John F. Kennedy, the then Malcolm X famously said, "The chickens have come home to roost," the present situation of America's entanglement in Jihad is what he was envisioning.

"Islam" means "peace" in Arabic. It is important to remember this.

Songs of Hope: Harry and the Jehovah's Witnesses

I remember first and foremost the pool at the Ramada Inn—my first time in a swimming pool. And with white children. My half-brother and I were not the only black children in the pool that warm Saturday afternoon, but it felt bizarre and new and brave. Of course I had been going to integrated schools since the first grade and was no stranger to frolicking with white kids. But that had been limited to schoolhouses and weekdays, a rather controlled environment. This felt different, more intimate somehow. I remember Rodney getting cold, his face dappled with chlorinated-water, shivering but not wanting to get out, ever. And I remember my father Harry's smile, when it came time for us to leave. We went to a movie afterward, a Walt Disney feature, *The Apple Dumpling Gang Rides Again*. It was dumb and amusing, colorful, loud. I was fifteen and Rodney was ten. We were at a convention of Jehovah's Witnesses.

Though my father never directly proselytized to me, he did feel the need to expose me to his faith, this ur-American branch of Protestant Christianity second only to Mormonism in the extremity of its reinterpretation, reinvention of the white-steeple, choir-heralded, Old World religion. I honor his methodology, as laid-back and somewhat-hip as his laconic style. He would invite me to join him on certain Sundays at the Kingdom Hall, to this exotic place in Burgaw, North Carolina, which incidentally was the hometown of my great-grandmother, always a significant site for my family, resonant, historical. The Winesses' denominational approach to faith and religiosity appealed to me in a completely unexpected way, for it is a bibliocentric sect, fiercely dedicated to close textual readings (a presaging of my love of the New Criticism approach to literature). Their criticism of what they called "Christendom," i.e. everybody else, was bracing; it was my first exposure to an alternative to the prayer meetings, altar calls, fire-and-brimstone sermons, Eucharist of grape juice and wadded bread, Vacation Bible School and Sunday School, and full-throated, off-key choirs ("There is a fountain filled with blood / Drawn from Emmanuel's veins"), all of which were the backbone of my small, verdant world. The Jehovah's Witnesses, I would later think, closely resembled the Talmudic scholars of Yeshiva lore, the Book supreme, the interpretations textual, and the affect somber as all get-out. That unnerved me, in the end. The magazines *The Watchtower* and *Awake!* both seemed a bit cartoonish and manmade when compared to stained glass and the Nashville-produced leather Bibles I knew. The Witnesses' insistence upon the term "torture stake" over "cross" as the instrument of Christ's death seemed unaesthetic to my teenaged mind (The crucifix is a pretty commanding sight; iconic). Their interpretations of the Book of Revelations were particularly gruesome and elaborate—and they became an idee fixe for a fan of apocalyptic horror films; I had nightmares about the whore of Babylon and her oily thighs. Their fatalistic fixation on an obscure verse regarding 144,000: the number of saints who would enter Heaven, was ultimately quite depressing, like the odds of winning lotto. And the Kingdom Hall itself resembled a plusher version of the Quaker Meeting Halls, and it felt more like a library than a sanctuary.

But these were the impressions of a boy. I did not feel pressured to join, and I found the logistics of so doing hard to fathom, though I thought on it hard and often. Their version of what they proudly called "The Truth" held a certain fascination. Moreover, it had rescued Harry L. Kenan in a way that caused much joy among my kinfolk. My grandfather always gave the Witnesses the credit for my father's turn from outlaw to upstanding, hardworking citizen. He was an old-time Baptist himself, and I don't think he fully understood or cared to understand the theology of the Jehovah's Witnesses or spent much time worrying about it. For him they were just another denomination. As pragmatic as Rockefeller he: If it works it works.

So my weekend among the faithful, not my first exposure to them, was calm, uncontroversial, and enticing. The talks were not boring; the crowds—multiracial in a time long before I had been exposed to true diversity—intoxicating; and the time with my father and brother an adventure. The good cheer almost grated upon my country boy sense of rectitude; I had never been around so many white folk who treated me like one of the crowd. It was downright unsettling. I came away with an indelible image of another way. Something deeply affected my perception of religion as a whole.

I remember that upon my return to my quotidian, agrarian, junior high school existence Mr. Brown asked me about my weekend pilgrimage to then down-at-heel Greensboro and the convening of the faithful. I remarked that I had never seen so many happy people, black, white, Asian; that it had never occurred to me (I was fifteen) that folk could get along so well. Mr. Brown smiled and said, "They are of one accord." When people have the same idea, he said, when they have nothing to fight about, they can be like that. When you introduce difference, that's when things go awry.

• • • • •

At the turn of the twenty-first century my father became an Elder and a minister of his Kingdom Hall. I was not able to attend the ceremony—which I imagine was solemn though self-effacing and as anticeremonial as most things J.W.—for I was living in Memphis and could not make the trip. I wished I could have been there. I have a photograph of the aftermath, my father flanked by my great-aunt Mary Fleming, his father, his wife, and his stepmother. How odd that now he is the man of God and I am the sinner, the Christian agnostic apostate. But there is always hope in this vast and ecumenical Protestantism we Americans all swim in...

I often look to a poem by my fellow North Carolingian, a founder of the National Organization for Women, a civil rights lawyer, an organizer of the March on Washington, a poet and memoirist, and the first woman Episcopal Priest, Pauli Murray:

> Hope is a crushed stalk
> Between clenched fingers.
> Hope is a bird's wing
> Broken by a stone.
> Hope is a word in a tuneless ditty—
> A word whispered with the wind,
> A dream of forty acres and a mule,
> A cabin of one's own and a moment to rest,
> A name and place for one's children
> And children's children at last . . .
> Hope is a song in a weary throat.

When all is said and done, we are alone together. That is the human condition.

Perhaps my favorite of all James Baldwin's writing, out of his vast and unprecedented work, is, oddly, a profile he wrote in 1960 for *Esquire* magazine. In "The Northern Protestant" (originally entitled "The Precarious Vogue of Ingmar Bergman"), Baldwin travels to Sweden and hangs out with the great director, famous for his grim, dark, wise, insightful visions of Scandinavian life. *Wild Strawberries. The Naked Night. Smiles of Summer. The Seventh Seal.* On the face of it, Baldwin might have seemed a peculiar choice to send to Stockholm, where the master of cinema worked and led a rather austere life, largely isolated. But Baldwin was excited by the prospect of discussing not only Bergman's aesthetic and techniques, but the thing he recognized that they shared: Protestant Christianity. Baldwin saw beyond the distance, beyond the languages and the skin colors, to all the things he and Bergman had in common: both sons of repressive, stern, almost abusive men-of-the-cloth fathers, both troubled by negotiating relationships and sex and love in the light of Scripture, both writers and dramatists, both shaped—ultimately—by the tenets of John Calvin and by their Christ-haunted histories.

Before I read that essay I had felt that same unexpected kinship with Bergman's work, and I had seen, even more markedly in the many films he would go on to make after meeting Baldwin, how the Swede showed the soul, encased in a sin-prone body, trying to make its way back to some Godhead, some transcendence, some meaning, in this unforgiving and cold world full of traps and sensual joys, temptation like a cornucopia and death, death, death, grim, inexplicable, cleansing, mysterious, leveling death.

For the Left-leaning, liberal-minded humanists, it may be difficult to admit how much of the move toward a more perfect union, toward a nation built on the Dream more than the reality, has been built on religion, American religions, just as Benjamin Quarles had illuminated for me all those years ago. The debates and the arguments have always been cast in a moral light, and our best teachers of morality have always been the ancient prophets and some sense of a higher way, call it God's way or simply Love. It is hard to imagine that our future course will, or will be able to, diverge from that legacy, bloody, problematic, a thicket of disagreement and muddled thinking, and yet we are better off with that legacy than without it, and our journey will benefit from paying heed to that history.

In the Protestant camp, Yahweh is not seen as a trickster—all the major monotheistic religions share that view. Come the Judgement Day, both Brother Rabbit and Brother Fox will be judged, each to each, their agendas fallen by the wayside. Their souls laid bare, the only significant question will be: What did you do with what you had?

· · · · ·

Charles A. Tindley, born a slave, known by many as the father of American gospel music, wrote "I Shall Overcome" in about 1900, and the song went on to become a large part of African American church culture among more than 100 of his hymns. The first known occasion on which it was used as a protest song, as it has ever since been identified, was by tobacco workers on strike in 1945. Soon afterward, individual singers—mostly labor organizers and rabble-rousers against the powers that be—began using this song throughout the South and changed the lyric to "We Shall Overcome." Some wondered about the efficacy of changing the individual to the collective. Nowhere was this more passionately debated than at the famous activist Highlander Folk School in New Market, Tennessee. A discussion ensued among progressives, black folk and white folk, including the likes of folk singers Pete Seeger, Guy Carawan, Frank Hamilton, and activist/teacher Septima Clark. Among the black folk there was a sense that not only was the title simply a matter of tradition, but that it was presumptuous to speak for anyone other than yourself. Others, including many of the white folk, felt that a sense of unity and solidarity had to be unambiguous. This tension is telling, for in its way that high-minded back-and-forth underscores so much of the battle between the black and the white views of the world; an existential recognition of ultimate aloneness, and of a need for cooperation, for blending, for change. Fox and Rabbit must see eye to eye. For, indeed, together they decided.

But I is always in We, and We are every man and every woman. We each sing our own Sorrow Song.

Nevermore

Fly, Black Bird, Fly

Ron Brown wasn't the first Brother Raven on the scene. Surely they have been with us all along. Surely Olaudah Equiano, kidnapped at age eleven along the Niger River, taken as a slave on a ship where he learned everything, *everything*, about sailing, sold to a Caribbean plantation, achieving his freedom, establishing himself in London, becoming a prominent abolitionist, writing a memoir that still sings to this day of the possibilities of a human being alone and without anything—surely he was a raven, back in the 1740s and '50s and '60s and '70s and '80s until his death in 1797.

I think of Robert Smalls, a highly capable and intelligent black man, held in bondage in Charleston, South Carolina, who became an accomplished seafarer for his "owners," and who, during the Civil War, managed to smuggle his family and an entire ship behind Union lines; who went on to meet Abraham Lincoln, and was awarded by him for bravery, and who would go on to serve as a State Senator in South Carolina and then to represent that state in the United States Congress for five terms. Sometimes the word "possibilities" seems feeble.

Fox, rabbit, and more. He learned to fly. Perhaps the myth began with men like these. Took wing. A prophesy and a promise.

• • • • •

In these magical, vulnerable, anxious, Prozac-soothed and BlackBerry-distracted days, an entirely new class within a class is emerging, attracting little attention to themselves as black folk, yet wearing their blackness proudly, like an inherited and handsome overcoat against the weather, while sallying forth on their own particular missions, taking Americanness as their first agenda, standing before black folks and white folks alike. Wonder of wonders, they are accepted, embraced, beloved in a way unimaginable forty years ago. And unlike an old vision of the middle class, this one, as the columnist David Brooks likes to say, is a new upper class, bourgeois bohemian, ruled by meritocracy, education, and achievement. Perhaps forty years ago they might have made a wee dent in the American landscape as exceptional individuals, but it is unimaginable that they could have risen, achieved, and been accepted in the way that they have in this new millennium. Their number is legion, refreshingly, and it is growing. You see them every day, or hear them. I mention only a few in the vanguard:

I had read Malcolm Gladwell's pieces in the *New Yorker* as they appeared several times a year, looking forward to his curious way of approaching what often seemed to be the humblest of topics with flair and slow-fire provocation. His first book, *The Tipping Point*, is on its way to becoming one of the all time best-sellers. His second book, *Blink*, has become just as popular. In that book he uses himself to illustrate a point about his central thesis—the "science" of how humans make up their minds in the blink of an eye. He tells of a time when he cuts his long mop of hair, and how, after the haircut, people begin to treat him as a black person: His father is white, his mother is black. Is he black? (By law, in the U.S.A. he is a Negro—according to the famous "One-drop Rule," despite his being Canadian by birth.) To me, the amusing thing about Malcolm Gladwell is that his success has had nothing to do with his blackness, nor has that blackness barred him. He neither apologizes for it nor makes it a central part of his art. Forty years ago he would not have been allowed this nonchalant and intriguing freedom. And people who love what he does would have been denied his delicious wares.

What can explain Oprah Winfrey? She continues to bring more new questions than answers to that question. As the flotilla of her navy sails on, it grows and grows. Her universe is unprecedented, undreamt of, dismissed at the dismisser's peril. Oprah does not easily fit into the construct of the new race-free Negro because she has never tried to downplay her blackness; in fact, she has often gone out of her way to emphasize it. An elegant case in point would be her gala Legends' Weekends where she fêtes black women of exceptional accomplishment at her California mansion. I point to Oprah because she has been allowed to define her African Americanness in a way few have, much in the same way Queen Hatshepsut defined her gender: on her own terms.

Indeed, forty years ago (even twenty years ago) such a phenomenon as Ms. Winfrey and what she has established would have been pure fantasy. Oprah gets Americans to buy books, and, by Jesus, to read them; Oprah gets legislation passed; Oprah takes on an entire industry in a court case and wins; Oprah becomes a billionaire.... In many ways Oprah's power lies in how sparely and discriminatingly she uses her power.

One of Oprah's major secrets is that she can be a nonjudgmental sister-critic (not a mother, as some accuse) as well as her paradoxically vulnerable role-model self. She is the older sister who has your back, who is looking out for you; yet who can, with arms akimbo, tell you the painful truth about yourself ("You need to lose weight"; "You need to stop spending so much money with credit cards"; "You need to give more to charity"; "You should vote"), but with love, and not the fake, air kissing "love" so prominent in modern media, but collard-greens-and- pork-fat love, even if served on Vera Wang china with Cartier flatware. And, at the same time, the Mistress of Harpo, Inc., over-indulges people (free cars, free houses, swag galore, even for people who don't come to see the show), yet another proof of her almost reckless love, her genuine admiration, and her boundless caring. We love Oprah cause Oprah loves us.

But more important than the fact of Oprah is the idea of Oprah. Her very presence, day to day, before twenty million sets of eyeballs is an unavoidable bellwether of a New America. More than a symbol. This cat will not go back into that bag.

And what of Barack Hussein Obama? Surely, of all Americans of Color at this current time, he seems to soar the highest. Clearly he represents a new paradigm, both political and social; his very candidacy forces, brings to the fore, topics of discussion long banished to small seminars on college campuses and to rehab-therapy groups—topics about how white folk feel about black folk, about how black folk actually feel about how other black folk define themselves. He could well be the catalyst for both the end of the civil-rights movement as we knew it and the beginning of a new type of participation. I say this to make clear how important I believe Senator Obama is and will be.

Obama flies, without a doubt. But his magic, that voodoo that he do so well is bound up in blackness. Not despite, but because of. A certain romance attends him, an aura, a mystery—is he black or half-African? What does African African American mean? What does his stance on race mean to me? Some cynics believe that the senator's suave, Harvard-educated, silver-tongued presence makes him profoundly acceptable to white folk whose guilty consciences make them want to vote for a black candidate, but who aren't quite as liberal as they think they are and harbor a tiny bit of negrophobia somewhere at the bottom of their cookie jars. But that's cynicism for you. Much is also made of Obama's biracial background. Those who choose to see it like to see a metaphor for national unity between black and white—his very body has been racialized in a rare and, more often than not, positive way. With his two best-sellers, *Dreams from My Father: A Story of Race and Inheritance* (1995) and *The Audacity of Hope: Thoughts on Reclaiming the American Dream* (2006), Obama forces these issues, embraces the awkward subjects and asks us all to think about them. And he makes us smile when he asks. Then he asks us to do more.

In the dark backward and abysm of time, the writer Irving Wallace published a now seemingly forgotten novel, *The Man* (1964). In the book, inconveniently, soon after the vice president dies, the secretary of state kicks the bucket on a surgery table and the president is killed in Europe. Before the twenty-fifth Amendment was added to the Constitution (1967), the much-coveted presidency went next to the president *pro tempore* of the Senate, who, in Wallace's feverish and labyrinthine though safe saga happens to be a mild-mannered Negro minister from Michigan. After the inauguration, hell-on-earth ensues, with racists running riot, and riots running riot, and racial ghosts coming out of closets like ghouls at Halloween. If Irving left *any* racial material on the cutting-room floor, I'd be shocked. The book was made into a somewhat less daunting movie in 1972 staring the great James Earl Jones. Cracking the book's spine today, I am reminded afresh not only how much of a white-supremacist nation America once was, but how close this realistically written "speculative fiction" was to our reality.

And yet how far. If Senator Obama becomes the United States of America's first black president, it will not be because he is not black, but because he *is*. This fact does not make him any less a trickster figure, any less a Raven. His rise will resonate in a different way than that of the new and rising generation; he will be, oddly and interestingly, a debt paid. One of many due black folk.

History is on his side, for he necessitates a full-frontal gaze at the injustices perpetrated on black women and men, while daring white Americans to imagine, in an appealingly tangible way, a way forward. He does not slip the yoke and tell the joke, as the novelist Ralph Ellison once insisted must be the mechanics of every Negro who becomes a success in the white man's world, but instead hauls the yoke along with him, with us. He has no intention of allowing people to forget. There is too much capital in that.

In no place is this irrevocable change in black mobility so evident than in the U.S. military. In the wake of Hurricane Katrina, a national catastrophe of historic proportions, a time rife with nasty ironies, one of the most amusing was when Mayor Ray Nagin called Lieutenant General Russel Honoré, "This John Wayne dude." The Duke did not care much for black folk. When the American government seemed to be floundering, in stepped Honoré to take charge. He barked orders to his soldiers, but with that recognizable edge of tough love. He got results. For a brief and shining time he loomed like a real-life comic-book hero.

Lieutenant General Russel Honoré is by no stretch of the imagination unique—though perhaps he is as a personality—but certainly he is emblematic of a new type of military (preceded on the national scene by Colin Powell, the first black chairman of the joint chiefs of staff) and perhaps a glimpse into the next America, the new paradigm. The military is not the wide world, of course, despite its power within it and sometimes over it. But in 1948, when Harry S Truman, essentially by fiat, integrated (not desegregated, but truly integrated) the armed forces, he ushered in the most socially fluid subculture in American history. As a result the American armed forces have been a model of true social integration. More than an experiment, they have become a shining example of what could happen to the society at large. To be sure, these militarized arms of the Executive are not perfect, but they serve as an antidote to doubt. The fact that the towns and cities around military bases are the most integrated in the United States should not be a mystery.

Business is sometimes very like war. There among the spread sheets, annual reports, and sales meetings, meritocracy seems to be, or at least to be becoming, the order of the day. Since the 1980s rise of Kenneth Irvine Chenault to the presidency of American Express and CEO at the company in the mid-1990s (yes, indeed, the first Black CEO of a *Fortune* 500 company), hope for a crack in the legendary glass ceiling in American Industry has grown. And though there has not been a rush on black men and women to fill those positions, a handful have quietly taken such reins. Perhaps the most remarkable—for the lack of emphasis on his color—was Dick Parsons at what was then AOL-Time Warner, a media company larger than most countries.

What is more troublesome than a trickster? A brood of tricksters. That is what Howell and Elvira Wayans unleashed upon the world with their unstoppable, talented, and shrewd four sons and daughter (and grandson). The Wayans brothers are the most financially successful black filmmakers in history and on the toptier among all current filmmakers in terms of overall box-office income and number of films. Their *Scary Movie* franchise reigns as the most successful series of commercial films ever made by black Americans. Beginning with the razor-sharp, unprecedented, and irreverent humor of *In Living Color*, their sketch comedy show that reinvented sketch comedy decades ago, they have set out, led by big brother Keenan, like a latter-day Rothchild family, a Damon here, a Malcolm there, a Wayne here, to make satire that challenges both black and white myths and stereotypes. Many of their films are spoofs and outrageous comedies, but some serious deconstruction goes on beneath the foolishness. Moreover, their films and television shows are seen more by white folk than by black folk, leading one to believe that their agenda is having real effect.

In 2006, the Pulitzer Prize for criticism went to Robin Givham for her "witty, closely observed essays that transform fashion criticism into cultural criticism." The fashion editor of the *Washington Post* became known for calling out the vice president of the United States for being poorly dressed at important state ceremonies; and for praising the secretary of state for her dynamic fashion sense. ("She walked out draped in a banner of authority, power and toughness. She was not hiding behind matronliness, androgyny or the stereotype of the steel magnolia.") Givham applied the same panache to her observations of political leaders that she applied to fashion models, singers, and entertainment moguls. The refreshing thing—to me—was that her blackness was secondary to her audacious claim to fame.

Did you know that Elmo was black? The Sesame Street puppet looks mighty orange on the television screen, but behind the loveable creature is a black man whose career began at age twelve on local Baltimore TV. Kevin Clash took over the role of Elmo in 1985, taking what had been essentially a blank slate and turning the character into an Emmy-winning vehicle and a best-selling toy.

And, finally, consider what it must be like now for a man who as a boy spent most of his childhood dreaming of one day becoming a physicist; for a boy who considered Carl Sagan's *Cosmos* to be a Bible of sorts (both the TV show and the accompanying book), and who held Sagan in as high esteem as some do the president—consider how uplifting it is to now see astrophysicist Neil DeGrasse Tyson following in Sagan's footsteps. Not only has he taken New York's Hayden Planetarium, where he is director, to a bright new national level, but he follows hard and fast in the late Sagan's footsteps as a popularizer, entertainer, and hard-science-minded advocate for both science and humanity in his television appearances and bestselling books (*Death by a Black Hole: And Other Cosmic Quandaries*). For that boy to have had a Neil DeGrasse Tyson on the scene—a black man—would have made terms like empowerment and self-esteem seem puny. I do not mean to suggest that there were no black physicists in the 1970s, and God bless their souls, but it was difficult to find them. And, as one of the good doctor's biggest fans, I have not once heard anyone mention his ethnicity. A bold new world, indeed.

I pick these celebrated few out as being emblems of a new New Negro. As a child of the 60s and growing up in the 70s, I find the continually refreshing thing, the element that I cannot get over, is how little is made of their obvious and undeniable blackness. That long-ago time when *Ebony* would—and could—make a huge deal about the first African American to scale a new height, as the rest of us stood on the ground and looked up in awe and pride, seems now a bit beside the point, an old horizon. The new overcoming is to become singularly, dynamically, importantly a success, and not despite of or because of. One is not magically "colorless"; color simply becomes another element in the mix, ceases to be a barrier. With them, at last and truly, color simply doesn't apply.

Meanwhile and meanwhile. As happy as we might be over such a phenomenon, we need to be mindful that this egress has only been achieved by a few. This emerging way of being and seeing is the new challenge, and not a small one.

At the forefront of this battle—within what can now be nostalgically called the Black Community—are two distinct subsets: that of the new New Middle Class, a black intelligentsia given new and larger wings by meritocracy, owing much to the successes of the civil-rights movement, the very real gains of affirmative action, and their own pluck and luck; and that of the negro vox populi, the masses of black folk, Brother Rabbit still largely an underclass despite the gains of the last hundred and two score years, still underemployed, undereducated, underrepresented, undermedicated, high blood-pressured, and HIV-infected; still borne up through single-parent homes and ill-funded and ill-administered schools; still dying too young from gunshot wounds inflicted by their own brethren, still used as pawns by a media and by the political classes who care more about digits than people. By "political classes" I mean the politicians and top staff who are either in power or grasping at power; the lobbyists and pollsters, the think-tank intellectuals who try to influence policy, not only in the (in)famous Washington Beltway but in fifty state capitals and every large municipality from sea to shining sea. Quite a large and varied lot.

Despite the aforementioned and impressive leaps forward, we are always snatched back to the inner-city streets of Detroit and Baltimore, to the shrinking numbers of black farms in North Carolina and Florida, to the Death Row tears of growing numbers of black brothers. So much of Brother Rabbit's plight remains the same as if it were forty years ago, and in some cases it is worse. And yet, despair is so easy.

There is an old song whose writer is anonymous but that was made famous by the legendary composer Harry T. Burleigh:

> I don't feel no ways tired
> I come too far from where I started from
> Nobody told me the road would be easy
> I don't believe, He brought me this far
> To leave me

The struggle has been ever thus, that sense of weary feet but rested soul. To accept a bleak outlook in the face of so many triumphs seems churlish when our legacy is so full of degradation and suppression and despisal.

A change is afoot. It has been a long time coming, but its march is undeniable. I would go so far as to dub the new New Negro "Brother Raven." Unpredictable. With aspects of both Brother Fox and Brother Rabbit—usually the best of their attributes. The troublesome character flaw in his case is perhaps also a strength: being interested in and curious about everything. As the saying goes: Curiosity killed the cat, but satisfaction brought him back. And remember, unlike the cat, the Raven can fly.

"One Day When I Was Lost"

I was speaking with a friend recently about James Baldwin's friendship with Martin Luther King, Jr., and Malcolm X. Particularly about what it must have felt like to have been the last man standing among them; about how Baldwin essentially fled the country—again—not long after their deaths, and how easy it was to see that Baldwin was becoming more and more disillusioned with his country. *What will happen to all that beauty?* he continued asking himself, even as he grew older. The beauty he saw in the free, wild, aggressive, enterprising black men and women of the streets of Harlem he had so loved in his youth. What will happen to that in the coming storm? The prospects could not have seemed bright, even in the

1980s when he sojourned in his home country from time to time as a journalist and teacher.

On April 4, 1968, the day Martin Luther King, Jr., was assassinated, Baldwin was in Palm Springs, California, working on an adaptation of Alex Haley's *The Autobiography of Malcolm X* for Columbia Pictures. He was sitting by the swimming pool with the actor Billy Dee Williams and listening to an Aretha Franklin record when he got the call. Less than a month before, Baldwin, along with the actor Marlon Brando (a friend from Baldwin's youth and a civil-rights activist in his own right) had introduced King at a Los Angeles rally. He writes in *No Name in the Street*:

> We had first met during the last days of the Montgomery bus boycott—and how long ago was that? It was senseless to say, eight years, ten years ago—it was longer ago than time can reckon. Martin and I had never got to know each other well, circumstances, if not temperament, made that impossible, but I had much respect and affection for him, and I think Martin liked me, too. I told him what I was doing in Hollywood, and both he and Andrew [Young], looking perhaps a trifle dubious, wished me well....That day, for a moment, it almost seemed that we stood on a height, and could see our inheritance; perhaps we could make the kingdom real, perhaps the beloved community would not forever remain that dream one dreamed in agony.

He would see King one last time, in New York, at Carnegie Hall. That night, King happened to speak about the legacy and relevance of the late W. E. B. Du Bois. For the Reverend King it was taking a step closer toward embracing the late icon's more critical stances and toward acknowledging a profound debt owed to him.

Baldwin had had some success as a playwright, with two plays produced on Broadway (*The Amen Corner* and *The Blues for Mr. Charlie*), though neither was as successful as his dear friend Lorraine Hansberry's seminal play *A Raisin in the Sun*. However, Hollywood stymied him, courting him and singeing him at the same time. He and the studio tangled over casting (they wanted Sidney Poitier, he wanted Billy Dee Williams); they tangled over focus and content (he saw Malcolm as a tragic American hero, they wanted to stress the outlaw factor); they tangled over credits; Baldwin lambasted the studio in the press; the studio hired another writer to rewrite Baldwin's script, which was entitled *One Day When I Was Lost*. ("What one cannot survive is allowing other people to make your errors for you, discarding your own vision, in which, at least, you believe, for someone else's vision, in which you do *not* believe.")

By this stage Baldwin's views were becoming more radical, and he was involving himself (often with discomfort) with groups like the Black Panthers.

Baldwin had also known Medgar Evers, the charismatic NAACP leader, who was gunned down in his own front yard in Jackson, Mississippi, in 1963. So much political bloodshed in less than ten years—the Kennedy brothers, Evers, Malcolm, King, not to mention so many other toilers in the vineyards of civil rights—weighed on and haunted Baldwin. No wonder he spent more and more of his time in Turkey and France. No wonder his tone became more caustic, disparaging, impatient, dark.

It is interesting to compare his tone in *Notes of a Native Son* to that in his last book, *Evidence of Things Not Seen*, a book about the Atlanta child murders published in 1985. He was ever the child minister, the once and future prophet, and the concept of Love remained paramount to him, but the possibility of redemption seemed even more difficult, and the cancer of white folks' sin against black folk, against the world; their love of capital and dehumanization, seemed even harder to surmount. After all those years, all that work, all that blood.

When he went to visit the Honorable Elijah Muhammad in 1962, he remained skeptical but encouraged: "I felt very close to him, and really wished to be able to love and honor him as a witness, an ally, and a father. I felt that I knew something of his pain and his fury, and, yes, even his beauty. Yet precisely because of the reality and the nature of the streets... we would always be strangers, and possibly, one day, enemies."

It was as if he had begun as a prophet Daniel, full of miracles and light and hope, singing of God's salvation-to-come, and had ended his days as a Habakkuk ("Oh Lord, how long shall I cry out and thou wilt not hear! Even cry out unto thee of violence, and thou wilt not save!" Habakkuk 1:2), or an Isaiah full of eloquent dread, foretelling Yahweh's wrath and great cataclysm...

The beauty is still here, Jimmy, and it is more glorious, more dazzling, and infinitely more transforming than any of us could have dreamed. It's been a long time coming, but a change is gonna come, baby. Hold on. Curse me for a fool, but I think the time is now. I believe I am a witness. I've seen the ravens begin to take wing.

Acknowledgements

This book was the idea of my editor and publisher, Dennis Loy Johnson. I'd like to thank him for his encouragement and patience—especially patience.

Any mistakes found herein are solely my doing.

NCR   2-14